PAUL WEBB

Paul Webb has been a teacher and freelance copywriter.
Four Nights in Knaresborough is his first stage play. It was
premiered at the Tricycle Theatre in London, directed by
Richard Wilson with Jonny Lee Miller, James Purefoy,
Christopher Fulford and Martin Marquez as the four knights
and Mali Harries as Catherine. Miramax has begun production
of a major film written by Paul Webb and based on *Four
Nights in Knaresborough*. He is currently working on a new
Miramax film and a new stage play.

Other Titles in this Series

Paul Webb

FOUR NIGHTS
IN
KNARESBOROUGH

NICK HERN BOOKS
London
www.nickhernbooks.co.uk

A Nick Hern Book

Four Nights in Knaresborough first published in this revised
edition in Great Britain in 2001 as a paperback original by Nick
Hern Books Limited, 14 Larden Road, London W3 7ST

First published, under the name Paul Corcoran, in 1999

Four Nights in Knaresborough copyright © 1999, 2001
Paul Webb

Paul Webb has asserted his right to be identified as
the author of this work

Typeset by Country Setting, Kingsdown, Kent CT14 8ES
Printed and bound in Great Britain by Biddles Ltd, Guildford

ISBN 1 85459 498 2

A CIP catalogue record for this book is available from
the British Library

Preface

' . . . we've made the worst career move in history!'

Little is known about the four most famous assassins in English history. The facts are that on Christmas Day 1170, four knights – Reginald FitzUrse, William de Traci, Richard le Bret and Hugh de Morville – left Henry II's court in Normandy and four days later killed Archbishop Thomas Becket in Canterbury Cathedral. They ran north and holed up in Knaresborough Castle. For a year.

Two things struck me about the four knights. In the literature concerning the struggle between Henry and Becket the knights have been strangely neglected. They're the ones who did the job, after all. And there's the year in Knaresborough Castle. That was a long time for four powerful men to stare at the walls, each other and the total ruin they had just made of their careers. What went on between them? We can only begin to imagine.

The popular imagination tends to simplify and distort history. Above all it patronises, implicitly assuming that our predecessors are somehow lesser. Doubting we can learn from our inferiors we simply fail to take the past seriously enough. Paradoxically, *Four Nights In Knaresborough* is a comedy – a fact which took me completely by surprise when I started writing it. The comedy stems from the knights' bitter awareness of a catastrophic error on a scale so grand it's absurd. But I also wanted them to convey some of the immense energy, intelligence and achievement of the twelfth century. They are decidedly our equals.

So much for my attitude to the characters but clearly the play could not avoid the big question. Why did they do it? The popular version – four outraged soldier-aristocrats decide to butcher Becket without the king's knowledge – seems inadequate. A more convincing and interesting account is given in Frank Barlow's standard biography *Thomas Becket*. They went to Canterbury with the king's knowledge to present

Becket with an ultimatum and, if he rejected it, to arrest him.
They under-estimated Becket's popular support in England, his
physical courage and his willingness to die. The question to
which no facts are available is what role was played by the
knights' personalities and private motives? This was to me the
most interesting question of all. *Four Nights in Knaresborough*
offers an imaginary answer.

Paul Webb

*There are two sets, both of similar character. The first is a
Norman chapel. The second is a room in Knaresborough Castle.*

*Four nights, spanning the year in Knaresborough, provide the
play's action and structure.*

ACT ONE

Morville's Dream

Scene One
Scene Two

Knaresborough Castle

Night One: January 1171
Scene Three: evening
Scene Four: later that night

Night Two: March 1171
Scene Five: evening
Scene Six: an hour later

Interval

ACT TWO

Scene One: early hours of next morning

Night Three: September 1171
Scene Two: evening
Scene Three: later that night

Night Four: December 1171
Scene Four: morning
Scene Five: that night

Four Nights in Knaresborough was first presented at the Tricycle Theatre, London on 4 November 1999, directed by Richard Wilson, with the following cast:

TRACI	Christopher Fulford
CATHERINE	Mali Harries
FITZ	Martin Marquez
BRITO	Jonny Lee Miller
BECKET/WIGMORE/VISITOR	Alan Parnaby
MORVILLE	James Purefoy

The play was revived, in the version published here, for a national tour, in September 2001, directed by Paul Miller, with the following cast:

TRACI	Robert Cavanah
CATHERINE	Joy Brook
FITZ	Tim Dantay
BRITO	Nick Moran
MORVILLE	Joseph Millson

The casting of the parts Wigmore, John the Visitor, and Becket was not confirmed at the time of going to press.

Characters

BRITO, *early twenties*

FITZ, *mid-thirties*

MORVILLE, *about thirty*

TRACI, *early thirties*

CATHERINE, *mid-twenties*

THE BOY, *Catherine's son, ten*

BECKET, *fifty*

WIGMORE, *fifty*

JOHN, THE VISITOR, *fifty*

ACT ONE

Scene One

Morville's Dream

Plainsong. It increases in volume as light gradually reveals a low-vaulted Norman chapel. Upstage is a bare altar. There are four effigies of crusader knights – two on each side of the stage.

In front of the altar BECKET *kneels at prayer. The singing rises in volume, intensifying in beauty.* BECKET *crosses himself, stands and turns. Robed in full archiepiscopal splendour, he's an impressive, even supernatural, sight.* BECKET *walks between the effigies towards the audience, stopping centre-stage. Snare drums emerge from behind the singing. The harsh rattle of the drums gets stronger until the plainsong is effaced and a powerful, driving tattoo fills the auditorium – so loud, finally, that it's oppressive. The drum climaxes and ceases.*

A stained glass window showing the head of a stern God – a Jehovah – bursts into light. BECKET *and the surrounding stage are bathed in colour. The silence intensifies.*

The four effigies sit up in one quick movement to become four KNIGHTS. *They stare at the monk for several moments then stand, draw their swords, step forward and kneel in a tight circle.*

FITZ. The King!

MORVILLE. The King!

TRACI. The King!

BRITO. The King!

ALL. The King!!

    They stand and move downstage towards BECKET.

MORVILLE. Traitor!

FITZ. Rabble rouser!

TRACI. Posturer!

MORVILLE. Treasoner!

FITZ. Upstart!

TRACI. Egotist!

MORVILLE. Reactionary!

BRITO. You . . . *fuckwit!*

A brief silence.

MORVILLE. No, Brito.

MORVILLE *steps closer to* BECKET *and contemplates him.*

The son of a shopkeeper who becomes Chancellor of the Exchequer *and* Archbishop of Canterbury is no 'fuckwit'.

The others move up alongside MORVILLE.

FITZ. Four days ago, on Christmas Day, you excommunicated the Bishops of York, London, Salisbury, Chester and Durham. The king demands their reinstatement. Now. Well?

BECKET *shakes his head.*

Then you're under arrest. The charge is treason.

MORVILLE. You must allow us to escort you to Normandy to be tried in the king's court.

BECKET *shakes his head.*

FITZ. So be it!

FITZ *steps up to* BECKET *and raises his sword.*
MORVILLE *stops him.*

MORVILLE. What are you doing?

FITZ. He's resisting arrest!

MORVILLE. Resisting? All he's done is shake his head! Let's just get him out of here!

FITZ. And then what?

MORVILLE. Take him back!

FITZ. Not without free passage! Look at us! After three hours sleep in three days it's a fucking long way to the channel, Morville!

BRITO. What do you think, Traci?

FITZ. What Traci thinks doesn't matter, Brito! *I'm* the one Henry instructed.

MORVILLE. To arrest him!

FITZ. To get a *result!* Running back to Normandy with nothing – leaving him here – alive – is *not* a *result!*

BRITO. What do you think, Traci?

TRACI *is still for a moment. He sighs.*

TRACI. Morville. Are you willing to face the king empty-handed?

MORVILLE *is silent.*

No. So this is the situation. His support in this country is beyond belief. Drag him across Kent to the channel and we could spark off a rebellion. Even the rabble gathering in the nave could present problems. Much longer we might not get out of the cathedral. (*Pause.*) If he won't come with us . . . he has to die. Now.

TRACI *moves towards* BECKET, *quickly shadowed by* BRITO *and* FITZ. *Silence.*

Thomas. There's no more time. Tell your men you're going to Normandy. It'll be the trial of the century. You'll be brilliant and you'll love every moment. Come to Normandy.

BECKET *shakes his head.*

FITZ. Then go to hell!

FITZ *steps forward, raising his sword, with* TRACI *and* BRITO *half a pace behind him. An explosion of light and noise is followed by blackout. Drums carry through to the next scene.*

Scene Two

Morville's Dream.

MORVILLE *appears front of stage. The snare drums are there throughout, as if urging him on.*

MORVILLE. If you were an ambitious thirty-five year-old repressed homosexual with a flair for economics and a good-looking twenty-one year-old genius of a king lifts you out of obscurity to give you power and wealth beyond your dreams! . . . Well, you'd fall in love with him wouldn't you? I'd have gone gay on the spot! At a stroke Becket became the second most powerful man in the kingdom. Chancellor of the Exchequer and Henry's closest adviser. They achieved many things but Henry's greatest desire – a legal system based on equality – one law for one people! – was denied him, because the Church claims the right to try *its* people – anybody from a bishop to a gravedigger! – in its own courts. Church courts are a grotesque pantomime. *Priests* can get away with murdering not just each other but their parishioners! Degenerates flock to take up the cloth – to enjoy a lifetime of depravity! That's why Henry asked Becket to become Archbishop. To help him reform a corrupt and criminal Church. Becket accepted, became Archbishop – and overnight turned into a raving fundamentalist, a vicious reactionary – opposed to any change no matter how small. And this for the man who'd given him the *world!* (*Pause.*) Why? Because over the years he'd turned *sour!* Sour with the knowledge that greatness is beyond love, that though Henry *cares* for everyone he *loves* no-one. *Needs* no-one. So Becket fell in love with someone else. Himself! With the utterly fantastic creation he made of himself as defender of the Church, as God's most loyal lieutenant and, finally – and he *wanted* this, oh yes – England's most glorious martyr. Not an easy thing to do. To change from the man he was – the man who loved the glory of war, who led an army against the French and defeated their champion in single combat, whose displays of wealth and status overawed kings! – to change from that man to a half-starved ascetic stitched into a lice-infested vest, that required an intensity of purpose that would consume ordinary people like us.

Put that man's self-discipline and will in my body and I'd disappear in a puff of smoke. What a *waste!* What a waste of talent and courage! Think what he could have done if he'd kept faith with Henry and with *progress!* Remember the anarchy when criminal gangs roamed the land at will? Today a woman, possessing virginity and carrying gold, can walk the length of England unaccompanied – and lose neither! Henry made England safe for ordinary people. Henry created the finest system of government since the Romans. Henry introduced the jury system. Reformed the tax system. Founded schools and universities. *Henry . . . is* a genius. A genius who's building a new world of order, prosperity and peace. For all of us! To kill a traitor to such a leader requires no examination! Many would claim it as a privilege. I claim it only as a duty! To my king – and his people! (*Pause.*) An extraordinary man must die – because he opposes the work of a *great* one!

The drum builds and continues through the scene change.

Scene Three

Knaresborough Castle.

January 1171.

The drum. A bare stone-built room. There's a cavern of a fireplace at the right, containing a feeble fire. At the back in the centre is an archway leading to rising stairs. On the left, a simple door. High up is a small, circular stained glass window – which remains dull and virtually unlit. A large table bears meagre quantities of cold meat, bread, a large jug of wine, plates and cups. Swords and axes are placed strategically about the room, at the ready.

MORVILLE *is sitting asleep in front of the fire, sideways on to the audience. He's whimpering in the midst of a nightmare. The drumbeat fades and* MORVILLE's *whimperings become clearly audible.*

BRITO *surveys the table and nurses his jaw. He pours some wine into a cup. From off there's a long roar of pain – which* BRITO *ignores.* BRITO *turns to* MORVILLE *and watches him curiously as his whimperings turn to small cries.*

BRITO. Morville. (*Pause.*) Morville!

BRITO *sighs and walks over to him.*

MORVILLE. Come to Normandy! . . . Come with us! . . . Come with us! . . . No!!

MORVILLE *cries out in despair. At the same time* BRITO *gives him a casual shove. He wakes.*

MORVILLE. Ah! Ah! . . . Ah . . . Ohh . . . Brito.

MORVILLE *gives an enormous sigh of relief.*

Oh . . . Brito. I was . . .

BRITO. Having a nightmare. I know. (*Pause.*) Do you want some wine?

MORVILLE *shakes his head.*

MORVILLE. It wasn't a nightmare.

BRITO. No.

MORVILLE. It was a dream.

BRITO. Yes. Same one?

MORVILLE. No.

Silence.

Same beginning – we're dead, we're effigies, we come to life, but this time . . .

Silence.

BRITO. What?!

MORVILLE. This time . . . after we killed him . . . or was it before? – before! – I . . . *was* it after we killed him? Or before? . . .

BRITO. Fuck's sake, Morville. *What?*

MORVILLE. What do you mean 'what'?

BRITO. What the fuck *happened?! This* time!

MORVILLE. I gave this speech in the cathedral. Explaining. Why we did it. Or were going to do it. Anyway, it was masterful. Why is it you can talk so brilliantly in dreams but not in real life?

BRITO. Because in real life you're a boring old fuckwit.

MORVILLE. But all the same words are in here. (*Touches his head.*) They must be. It was so clear. And so convincing.

BRITO. And so long?

MORVILLE. What?

BRITO. Was it a long speech?

MORVILLE. Enormous. But by the end of it everyone knew exactly why he had to die.

BRITO. By the end of it the only thing they wanted to know was when.

A long silence. MORVILLE *stares at the fire.*

Christ it's cold!

Silence.

Don't you think it's cold in here?

Silence.

Christ I do. I'm freezing.

Silence.

That fire is pathetic. If a passing sparrow shits down the chimney, that's it. We're finished. 'What happened to the four knights who murdered Becket?' 'Oh them. Poor fuckers froze to death in Knaresborough Castle.'

Silence.

My balls feel as if they're about to shatter into a thousand pieces. Don't you think it's cold? Wake up! Talk to me!

MORVILLE *raises his head and looks at* BRITO.

Do you or do you not think there's a chill in the air?

MORVILLE. It's the middle of January.

BRITO. Exactly! Exactly, Morville! You've cracked it! It's the middle of January! So organise that sour-faced bitch and let's get some decent firewood in here!

Silence followed by a cry of pain from off and a plea: 'Oh dear God – help me!'

And why am I doing all the complaining? It's your castle
and your guests are dying of exposure – *inside* the place!

Silence.

MORVILLE. You need activity. Find something to do.

BRITO. I've *done* enough! Since Christmas Day I've crossed
the channel in a hurricane, murdered an archbishop, ridden
day and night for three weeks across a country whose entire
population has one ambition: to roast my bollocks over an
open fire! (*Pause.*) It's been a stressful time, Morville. I'm
due a rest. But no. I've got toothache. I'm sleeping badly.
I've lost weight. I'm weak as a kitten. And no wonder.
I haven't had a decent meal in three weeks!

*BRITO takes a drink and recoils with a gasp of pain. He
holds his jaw.*

MORVILLE. Is it bad?

BRITO. Bad enough!

A roar of pain and anguish from off.

This English wine is piss. Is *piss!* If it weren't for this tooth
I wouldn't touch the stuff. It tastes like poison.

MORVILLE. Why do you think I'm not drinking it?

*BRITO stares at MORVILLE. He looks into his cup. He
sniffs it.*

BRITO. Bollocks. Three days and it hasn't killed me yet.

*He smells the wine again. Silence. BRITO picks up a sword
and does a few half-hearted exercises.*

You've never been a very happy person have you? (*Pause.*)
Have you?

MORVILLE. Happiness is a word for children.

BRITO. Ohh. . . ! You know your problem? You think being a
morbid git is a sign of superior intelligence. It isn't!

*BRITO gasps and holds his jaw for a few moments. A roar
of pain from off: 'Oh sweet Christ help me!' BRITO turns
towards the noise off and shouts.*

Hurry up and die!

BRITO *steps up to* MORVILLE *and points the sword at him.*

I know what's wrong with you.

Silence.

You're depressed.

MORVILLE *raises his head.*

MORVILLE. Whatever gave you that idea?

BRITO. Any man who freezes in his own house without a whimper is depressed.

Another roar of pain and defiance from off: 'Aagh, you bastard! Out! Get out*!'*

MORVILLE. Excommunication is only the beginning. You do realise that don't you? You do realise we've made the worst career move in history!

BRITO. I don't care! I *care* to get warm. To get rid of this toothache. To eat.

MORVILLE. God knows what penance the Pope will demand.

BRITO *starts towards the arch.*

BRITO. A good hard shag is what the Pope would order right now. 'Go forth from this place, my son, and put it about. Give several a *large* portion.'

BRITO *exits. After a few moments,* CATHERINE *enters by the door, carrying a jug. She's upright, shapely and strong. She carelessly places the jug on the sideboard and walks quickly back towards the door.*

MORVILLE. Catherine.

CATHERINE *stops, turns and gives* MORVILLE *a contemptuous glare.*

CATHERINE. Yes? My lord?

MORVILLE. Catherine . . . you've got to start . . .

CATHERINE. Yes?

MORVILLE. Showing more respect.

CATHERINE. Respect!

MORVILLE. The others don't . . . understand. They think I'm weak.

CATHERINE. You are! How else did you allow yourself to follow these murderers – and *fools!*

MORVILLE. I haven't followed anyone. We're all equals in this.

CATHERINE. All equally sinful and equally stupid. Look at you. A prisoner in your own castle!

MORVILLE gets out of the chair and walks over to stand close to CATHERINE.

MORVILLE. Kate! For Christ's sake! If you go on like this it'll give me serious problems. They've been patient so far. But DeTraci and FitzUrse are powerful men with large households. They're not used to being treated with contempt by their servants!

CATHERINE. I'm not their servant.

MORVILLE. No. You're mine. And they are my guests! (*Pause.*) One of them will lose his temper with you and . . .

CATHERINE. And?

MORVILLE. And I'll have to defend you.

Silence.

Oh . . . Kate . . . I . . .

CATHERINE. You've done so well for yourself since you left, haven't you?

MORVILLE. Oh, so now we have it.

CATHERINE. A member of the royal household. Once.

MORVILLE. *I* didn't marry!

CATHERINE. Just as well! Any wife of yours would die of shame.

Silence. MORVILLE begins to reach out to her but hears someone approaching. They turn to see BRITO enter through the arch. He's wearing an enormous fur-lined coat with the hood up. He looks absurd.

There's a brief moment between the three of them before CATHERINE heads for the door and exits. BRITO stares at MORVILLE, *waiting briefly for a reaction. But then there's another long roar of pain from off: 'Aaagh! Out you bastard! Get out!'*

MORVILLE *returns to his chair in front of the fire.* BRITO *doesn't move. He glances around the room.*

BRITO. What did she bring? (*Pause.*) Wood? Food? (*Pause.*) Anything?

MORVILLE. Water.

BRITO. Oh thank God. I don't mind freezing. I don't mind starving. But I'd just *hate* to die of thirst!

BRITO *picks up a sword.*

Why won't you use your authority? She's your *housekeeper* for God's sake!

BRITO *prods him with the sword.*

MORVILLE. I have no authority!

MORVILLE, *very angry, gets up from the chair, face to face with* BRITO.

None of us has any authority any more! (*Pause.*) Brito. I know you're very young and therefore very stupid but try, please try, to understand. All we have is a handful of soldiers whose loyalty is based on one thing – fear of what the mob might do to *them* if they allow the mob to take *us*.

They stare at each other briefly. MORVILLE *turns away and drops into his chair.* BRITO *props the sword exactly where it stood before. He returns to the sideboard and struggles for several seconds to cut some very stale bread.* BRITO *throws the bread-knife aside and holds up the bread.*

BRITO. I'm starving. But it hurts to eat. Soup would kill me, and what have I got?

BRITO *slams the loaf down on the breadboard.*

MORVILLE. I'll talk to Catherine about the tooth.

BRITO. What? Let that nightmare loose in my mouth? With instruments of torture? She'd love that!

BRITO *strides over to the sword, picks it up and returns to the sideboard. He raises the sword over the bread.*

I don't trust her. She'd probably kill me.

MORVILLE. She's the only reason any of us are still alive.

BRITO. If this bread damages this sword I will break down and cry.

MORVILLE. Catherine is personally cooking every bit of food that comes into this room.

BRITO *hits the loaf with the sword.*

BRITO. What? Like this stuff?

BRITO *holds up the sword. The loaf is stuck to it. He's beginning to lose his temper.*

Did she bake it – or just quarry the fucking thing?

BRITO *kicks the loaf off the sword onto the floor. At the same time* CATHERINE *enters, carrying firewood in a basket. She stops, watching* BRITO. *He doesn't notice her.*

Fuck! Fuck!!

He stamps on the loaf repeatedly.

Fuck! You fuck! Fuck! Fuck!!

He wrenches a small axe from the depths of his clothing and drops to his knees.

You fucking . . . fucking . . . loaf!!

BRITO *hacks at the loaf. There's another roar of pain from off.* BRITO *stops pulverising the loaf and, turning, shouts with all his force.*

Hurry up and die you noisy bastard!

He sees CATHERINE. *Silence. He's embarrassed.* CATHERINE *gives him an icy stare then walks imperiously across the room to the fireplace.* BRITO, *still on his knees, eyes her every movement with resentment and lust.* CATHERINE *carelessly drops the wood in the fire grate and turns to* MORVILLE. *Behind her,* BRITO *silently mouths her words in advance.*

CATHERINE. Do you require anything else . . . my lord?

BRITO *mouths* MORVILLE's *reply.*

MORVILLE. No thank you Catherine.

MORVILLE turns to the fire to avoid her look of anger and contempt. She turns and strides towards the door.

BRITO. Catherine.

As BRITO *gets wearily to his feet, returning the axe to his tunic,* CATHERINE *stops and turns towards him with barely concealed hostility.* MORVILLE *looks up apprehensively.*

CATHERINE. Yes? My lord?

BRITO. Is there a shortage of wood in this area?

CATHERINE. No.

BRITO. I thought I spotted a small forest out there. In fact, trees as far as the eye can see.

CATHERINE. Yes? My lord?

BRITO. Which leads me to ask a question, that's all. Why do you keep that fire on the edge of extinction?

CATHERINE. I'm not sure what you mean.

BRITO. I mean there's a million trees out there so why can't we have about ten decent sized logs in here? On that fire? Dry ones!

CATHERINE. It's difficult to get more without arousing suspicion and hostility.

BRITO. I'm cold, Catherine. I'm cold!

CATHERINE. It's the middle of winter and this is Yorkshire my lord.

BRITO. I know that! The grey, grey days that never even begin, the dampness that eats into your heart, the wine that makes vinegar seem like champagne, and the nights! The black nights that go on . . . all fucking night! And day! These things tell me it's winter and it's Yorkshire. But they don't explain why I have to be so *cold!*

CATHERINE. Perhaps you lack warm clothing my lord?

BRITO. I can hardly stand up for warm clothing! Look at me! My armour weighs less!

CATHERINE (*to* MORVILLE). May I go?

BRITO. Catherine. Listen to me. I beg you. I'm cold and I'm in pain. Please bring us more wood. Failing that –

BRITO *picks up the loaf.*

– bring us more bread.

BRITO *hurls the loaf into the fireplace.*

It burns a lot better than the wood!

CATHERINE *gives* BRITO *a look of intense dislike, turns and goes out through the door.*

What is it with you and that woman? Just tell her to bring some fucking firewood!

MORVILLE. Alright! Let me tell you about that woman.

MORVILLE *gets up and moves about.*

She is not my housekeeper. She isn't anybody's housekeeper. She owns one of the largest estates in the area, but because she's very bright and highly educated, and because she prefers administration to farming, she rents her estate and works here as my steward. She runs half the bloody county! *Now* – because of us – and because she *chooses* to help us – she's a housekeeper. But she can't bring waggonloads of food, drink and firewood in here because she's told people out there we're racked with remorse, in constant prayer and fasting. If they suspect we're sitting round a roaring great fire getting pissed and eating three square meals a day the likelihood of rebellion would become a certainty! (*Pause.*) Our lives hang by a thread, Brito. That woman *is* the thread.

MORVILLE *sits down again.*

It's difficult for her. And dangerous. Just . . . be patient.

BRITO *pretends not to have heard a word.*

BRITO. I think I should shag some respect into her. What do you think? Do you think I should shag some respect into her?

MORVILLE *jumps to his feet and grabs* BRITO.

MORVILLE. Go near her and I'll defend her with my life! And yours!

BRITO *isn't angry so much as impressed and curious.*
MORVILLE *begins to back off.*

BRITO. *Now* I get it. Of course. You . . . and her!

TRACI *enters through the archway.* MORVILLE *quickly turns away and sits down.* TRACI *is triumphant.*

TRACI. Good news men!

BRITO *is immediately cheered by* TRACI*'s presence.*
BRITO *pours wine into two cups.*

Piles, yes – and most of my arse is now at the bottom of the moat. But I am no longer constipated!

MORVILLE. What a load off all our minds.

BRITO. Whingeing I put up with. But toilet puns – no, Morville, *no!*

BRITO *hands* TRACI *the cup.*

TRACI. Thanks. How's the tooth?

BRITO. Not as bad as the wine. Or the cold. Or the company.

TRACI *looks closely at* BRITO.

TRACI. You look terrible. It'll have to come out.

BRITO. Maybe.

TRACI *drinks.*

TRACI. Good god!

He peers into the cup.

BRITO. Morville reckons it's poisoned.

TRACI. Poison?

TRACI *drinks.*

No. Tastes too bad.

TRACI *and* BRITO *laugh, touch cups and drink.*

What a place this is! The wind whistling up that latrine!
Ten minutes more and I'd still be there – frozen to the seat.
I've been in some desperate situations but that in there took more courage than most. I sat there, locked in mortal combat, eyes popping out of my head, sweat running down my face,

frost forming on my arse, an hour of gut-twisting effort –
and what did I have to show for it? A tiny nodule of
polished granite. The tip of a monstrous turd. I knew if I
took one breath it'd be straight back up there and no chance
of seeing it again for the rest of the day. So. With the faith
of a devout, the concentration of a trained philosopher, the
courage of a warrior knight, I persevered. Finally, after . . .
must have been, oh, five full minutes without a breath . . .
I was dying, I was definitely on the edge of unconsciousness,
when suddenly . . . it was out! I sat there, gasping with joy,
like a woman who's given birth to a gigantic child. And
then . . . I heard it. The sound of breaking ice. It was the
monstrous turd! By the time it reached the moat it had
frozen solid. Hit the ice and went straight through. Smack!
Steam . . . a little gentle bubbling . . . then all was still. And
mine arse was once more mine own.

BRITO. Congratulations, Traci! Here's to your noble arse.
Welcome back!

TRACI. For which, Brito, much thanks.

They drink and groan simultaneously.

BRITO. Hit the ice and went straight through? Bollocks.

TRACI. Go and have a look. All you'll see is a hole in the ice.

MORVILLE. Oh for Christ's sake you two.

TRACI (*to* BRITO). What's the matter with him?

BRITO. De Morville is De Pressed.

TRACI. Depressed? What have you got to be depressed about?

MORVILLE. Just the fact that we committed what people
think is the second murder after Christ.

TRACI. They'll get over it.

MORVILLE. When? It's been a thousand years since the
crucifixion and people are still killing Jews.

TRACI. Becket wasn't the son of God.

MORVILLE. No. But any day now someone will discover he
was. (*Pause.*) Look, you two. I've been excommunicated.
I'm a prisoner in my own castle. I expect any moment
someone sent by a king I worship to come through that door

and assassinate me. All that I can accept. But having to listen to two intelligent men talk endlessly about a turd! Now that is depressing!

Silence. BRITO *exits through the arch.*

MORVILLE. Henry has vowed to do penance in Canterbury. The king is to be scourged in public by monks.

TRACI. Those Canterbury degenerates couldn't drag themselves away from the table long enough. (*Flaring into anger.*) Scourge the king? Those guzzling pigs!?

TRACI *pauses to calm down.*

The king will stand by us. We're his men. King's men!

MORVILLE. The king can't stand by us. We kill a reactionary lunatic and the whole country behaves as if we gang-raped the Virgin Mary. Even Henry can't ignore popular feeling of that intensity. The sooner *someone* gets to us and kills us the better for Henry.

TRACI. No. I've been thinking about it in there. Between contractions. Listen to me, Morville. Henry is utterly alone in a sea of outrage. The last thing he can do right now is defend us. But he could try to make scapegoats of us. 'They're a bunch of criminal lunatics acting alone!' So why's he not done that? Because he knows it's totally incredible to anyone with half a brain. This is still about what it's always been about – a power-struggle between Henry and the Pope. Any move he makes against us will be interpreted as weakness. And not just by the Pope. By every one of his enemies.

BRITO *re-enters.*

Consider this also. Henry has repeatedly accused Becket of treason. Henry can't condemn us on the one hand without compromising with treason on the other. The man has many strengths – but compromise isn't one of them. Henry won't move against us. Nor will he want the mob to do so. His authority would be badly damaged if four of his knights were just taken out and killed. The problem is he's currently powerless to prevent it. The threat we face is all around us. The king is still our friend. Our only friend.

BRITO (*solemnly, to* MORVILLE). <u>He's right you know.</u>

MORVILLE. No. <u>He's wrong.</u>

BRITO. No he's bloody right! It went straight through. No sign of a turd! Just a big hole in the ice!

MORVILLE. Oh my god. No more – please!

TRACI. Actually, I lied. It didn't go straight through.

BRITO. I knew it!

TRACI. It hit the ice, bounced forty feet in the air, and then went through at the second attempt.

BRITO. Christ it's a miracle! You hear that Morville? A bouncing turd! It must be a sign!

MORVILLE. Enough! Please! I've spent three weeks listening to you talk utter crap –

BRITO. I warned you Morville! One more toilet pun –

MORVILLE. Please! Please! I'm becoming very worn down by it!

Silence.

You two won't be passing the time making jokes when you're fighting for the cross in Palestine the rest of your lives.

TRACI. Ooh. Gravitas from our host. So what's wrong with Palestine? Apart from plague, flies and lousy food. Personally, I could do with a change.

BRITO. At least it's warm.

MORVILLE. Suffering makes the strong stronger, Brito. It destroys the weak.

BRITO. Ooh. Profundity from our host.

TRACI. Is he saying you're weak? Shove his face in the fire and see what he says then.

BRITO. Shove *my* face in it. I'd say 'Thanks. Now do the rest of me.'

FITZ *enters by the arch.*

Hey Fitz. You heard about Traci's miraculous turd?

FITZ. Shut up, Brito.

BRITO. Oooh! Severity – from our 'leader'.

Silence.

FITZ. Look, boy! Let's get something clear. *They* are here on the king's recommendation to me. *They* are my social and military equals. *You* are here on Traci's whim. And you are not my equal. You're an ambitious little chancer from a dirt-patch tenancy on the Brittany border. Continue to provoke me and I'll put my boot up your arse – just to remind you who you are!

Brief silence.

BRITO (*quietly*). So long as it's only your boot.

The room is still. FITZ stares at BRITO. BRITO stares back. FITZ takes a step towards BRITO.

FITZ. What did you say?

TRACI. Who wants a steak the size of that table?

FITZ and BRITO ignore him for a few moments. Then BRITO grins and turns away to TRACI.

BRITO. Me! I want a steak the size of that table!

Silence. FITZ moves to the table.

FITZ. Where's the bread?

BRITO. I put it on the fire.

FITZ starts moving slowly towards BRITO.

FITZ. You did what?

BRITO. Put it on the fire.

FITZ. Why?

BRITO. Thought you might fancy some toast.

A brief pause, then FITZ gives BRITO a quick, sharp slap – on the side of the bad tooth. BRITO roars with pain. The pain intensifies and BRITO sinks to his knees, his fists clenched in front of his face.

MORVILLE. For Christ's sake, Fitz!

BRITO starts to get to his feet, aggressively. MORVILLE puts both hands on BRITO's shoulders.

Leave it!

BRITO *sinks to his knees again, groaning, exhausted by the pain.*

TRACI. This has gone on long enough. (*Pause.*) Can you find some pliers, Morville?

MORVILLE. Yes.

MORVILLE *exits through the door.*

BRITO. Where do you want me?

TRACI. In that chair.

BRITO *gets to his feet, walks across and sits in the chair.* TRACI *moves to stand in front of* BRITO.

Which one is it?

BRITO. This one.

BRITO *puts a finger into his mouth.*

TRACI. Right.

TRACI *feels for the tooth.* BRITO *recoils with a gasp.*

FITZ. I'd drink a bit more if I were you.

BRITO. Don't worry about me Fitz.

FITZ. I don't. It's just I'd rather not have to listen to your screaming.

BRITO. Why? Afraid it'll turn you on?

FITZ. If you say anything like that again –

BRITO. You'll do what, Fitz? Slap my face? Ooh, bitch!

TRACI *turns on* BRITO *with a powerful anger.*

TRACI. Be quiet you imbecile! Christ it's like living with a couple of rabid dogs! (*To* FITZ.) Ignore him! He's been drunk and in pain for days.

BRITO *shrinks beneath* TRACI*'s disapproval and turns away from* FITZ. MORVILLE *enters through the door, carrying a ridiculously large pair of pliers.*

BRITO. Fuck's sake!

BRITO *and* TRACI *are horrified.* FITZ *chuckles.*

I need a tooth pulled not my head torn off!

TRACI. Where'd you find those?

MORVILLE. The blacksmith. They're the smallest he had.

TRACI, *still angry, takes the pliers from* MORVILLE.

TRACI. Okay. Let's get it done.

MORVILLE. He's not drunk enough.

BRITO. I drink any more of that stuff I'll throw up.

TRACI. Okay. Open your mouth.

As carefully as he can, TRACI *puts the pliers into* BRITO*'s mouth and gets a grip on the tooth.* BRITO *shuts his eyes and his body goes rigid.* TRACI *places the palm of his left hand firmly on* BRITO*'s forehead. There's a pause then* TRACI *leans down hard on* BRITO*'s head with one hand while pulling with the other.* BRITO*'s hands grip the sides of the chair as he strains to hold his head back. He begins to emit a slow, quiet cry of pain and determination. Then there's a splintering sound followed by a rising scream of agony.* TRACI *lurches backwards.* BRITO *sits up, hands in front of his open mouth, head bowed in pain, gasping, blood beginning to flow from between his fingers.* TRACI *looks at the pliers and at the few splinters of tooth in its jaws.*

Have I got it?

BRITO *shakes his head.*

Fuck! Fuck! I'm sorry Brito.

BRITO. Get the rest of it! Now! Please!

BRITO *lies back, shaking and gasping. His hands grip the chair.*

TRACI. Morville! Come and hold him. Now! Now!!

MORVILLE *suddenly gets up from his chair and moves to* BRITO. *He takes* BRITO*'s head in his hands, leaning down on him.* TRACI *looks into* BRITO*'s mouth.*

MORVILLE. Come on, then.

TRACI. I can't see it. There's too much blood.

BRITO. Just do it!

TRACI *inserts the pliers.*

TRACI. Is that it?

BRITO *gives a strangled 'yes'.* TRACI *starts to pull. Again there's the sound of splintering and cracking. The pliers come away and* BRITO *gives a great howl.* MORVILLE *lets go of* BRITO*'s head.* TRACI *and* MORVILLE *look helplessly at* BRITO *while he twists his head from side to side, stifling cries of agony.* MORVILLE *strides to the door, throws it open and shouts through it with authority.*

MORVILLE. Catherine! Catherine! (*Pause.*) Kate!!

BRITO *grabs hold of* TRACI, *pulling himself upright. He leans his face against* TRACI, *gasping with exhaustion.* TRACI *tenderly holds* BRITO*'s head and shoulders as if he were a child.* FITZ *is no longer gloating but looks strangely desolate.*

TRACI. I'm sorry, Brito. I'm not very good at this am I?

BRITO *puts his head back and looks up at* TRACI, *gasping and weeping.*

BRITO. Fucking . . . useless!

CATHERINE *appears in the doorway.* BRITO *leans back in the chair and looks stupidly at her, blood running from his mouth, wincing as each breath passes over the tooth. After a shocked pause she walks quickly over to* BRITO.

CATHERINE. Let me see.

BRITO *opens his mouth.* CATHERINE *carelessly takes hold of his jaw. He yells with pain and pulls his head away.*

BRITO. Agh! You bitch!! Carefully!

CATHERINE (*to* MORVILLE). He's not drunk enough. Call me when he is.

CATHERINE *turns to go.*

TRACI. Catherine. He's as drunk as he can be without being sick.

She stops, turns and approaches BRITO *again.*

CATHERINE. Let me see.

BRITO *opens his mouth.* CATHERINE *takes hold of his jaw, gently this time.*

Well. You've crushed it. Where did you find those things?

CATHERINE *snatches the pliers from* TRACI *and throws them across the room.*

MORVILLE. Catherine!

CATHERINE *looks dismissively at* MORVILLE *then walks to the door. She pauses and turns briefly to* BRITO.

CATHERINE. Stay there.

CATHERINE *exits.* BRITO *hungers after her, breathing and gasping through clenched teeth.*

BRITO. I could shag that right now.

TRACI. No you couldn't.

BRITO. Yes. I could.

BRITO *points to his crotch.*

TRACI. No.

BRITO. Yes.

TRACI. You've got a hard-on?

BRITO *gestures 'touch and go, but yes'.*

There's something seriously wrong with you, Brito.

CATHERINE *enters carrying a small box and a bowl. Without pausing, she goes to the table and sweeps everything on it onto the floor.*

CATHERINE. Get him on the table.

CATHERINE *immediately moves on to the side table, puts down the box and bowl, fills a cup with water and puts it next to the bowl. Meanwhile* TRACI *and* MORVILLE *help* BRITO *onto the table.*

Lie down.

CATHERINE *turns to* TRACI, *pointing to the cup and bowl.*

Hold these.

TRACI *smiles sardonically at* BRITO *and* MORVILLE, *saunters over, picks up the cup and bowl and saunters back to the table. Meanwhile* CATHERINE *opens the box and takes out a small knife and a pair of pliers.*

CATHERINE (*to* FITZ). Pass these through the flames but don't let them get hot.

BRITO. No danger of that.

FITZ *collects the knife and pliers and takes them to the fire. CATHERINE comes over to the table and takes the cup of water from TRACI.*

CATHERINE. Wash your mouth.

BRITO *takes the cup from her and very carefully takes a mouthful. TRACI holds the bowl under BRITO's chin. BRITO opens his mouth and bloody water runs out of his mouth into the bowl. BRITO turns and looks at CATHERINE with a stare of defiance.*

Let me see.

BRITO *opens his mouth.*

Ah. That's better than I thought. Good. Lie down.

BRITO *hesitates.*

Lie down.

BRITO *lies down. CATHERINE begins to clamber onto the table and astride BRITO's legs. She moves herself along, until she is sitting astride BRITO's hips.*

BRITO. Oh Christ, it's almost worth it . . . !

CATHERINE. Give me the knife.

FITZ *gives her the knife.*

TRACI. What do you need the knife for?

CATHERINE. You've destroyed the tooth.

TRACI. Well?

CATHERINE. There's nothing to get a grip on.

BRITO. Oh yes there is.

CATHERINE. I need to cut the gum to expose more tooth.

CATHERINE *leans forward and looks into his mouth. The knife is at his throat. She looks into his eyes for a moment. BRITO's hands come up and grip her thighs.*

Take your hands off me.

He does so. CATHERINE *leans forward again and does some work with the knife in* BRITO's *mouth. It's quickly over.*

Wash your mouth.

CATHERINE *hands the knife to* FITZ *as* BRITO *sits up and takes the cup from* TRACI.

Give me the pliers.

FITZ *hands her the pliers.* BRITO *washes out his mouth.*

When you've done that open your mouth and lie back – quickly, before there's too much blood.

BRITO *nods his head, finishes emptying his mouth into* TRACI's *bowl and lies down.* CATHERINE *is immediately into his mouth with the pliers.* MORVILLE *leans down on* BRITO's *head.* BRITO *groans and tenses.* CATHERINE *has one hand braced on* BRITO's *chest. Their faces are very close.*

Right. I've got it. Hold him!

CATHERINE *starts to pull.* BRITO *cries out, this time like a young boy.*

Hold him!

TRACI *puts the bowl down and, with* MORVILLE, *helps to hold* BRITO *down.* BRITO's *hands come up and clamp onto* CATHERINE's *hips.*

Hold him! Hold him!

This is a tableau for several moments until, suddenly, the tooth is out. With a huge cry of relief, BRITO's *arched body slumps.* CATHERINE *sits astride him, gasping for breath, his hands still on her hips.*

They are all still for a while. CATHERINE *and* BRITO *look post-coital. Then* CATHERINE *slides off* BRITO, *gathers her instruments and exits by the door.* BRITO *gets shakily onto his feet.*

BRITO. Fuck. Fuck me. (*Pause.*) What a woman.

He takes a step, staggers and falls forward onto MORVILLE.

MORVILLE. Come on.

BRITO, supported by MORVILLE, moves towards the arch. He comes face-to-face with FITZ. There's a moment between them.

FITZ. Well done.

BRITO. Fuck off.

TRACI. Get him out!

They exit through the archway.

FITZ. That little shit is really beginning to irritate me.

TRACI. He irritates us all.

FITZ. I want you to stop him.

TRACI. Stop him?

FITZ. Irritating me.

TRACI. How can I do that?

FITZ. Easily. He idolises you.

TRACI. Does he?

FITZ. That's why he's here, isn't it? That's why he's so full of himself. He's with you and part of something major. The fact that it's a disaster doesn't matter to him – he's got nothing to lose in the first place.

Silence.

Look, Traci, it's bad enough without having to put up with constant provocation from a jumped-up apprentice. I want you to put the leash on him.

TRACI. I'll speak to him.

FITZ. You can do better than that.

TRACI. Why should I?

A pause. FITZ grins.

FITZ. You and I have been sharing the same whore. Did you know that?

TRACI. No I didn't. Have we?

FITZ. Yes. (*Pause.*) His name's Geoffrey.

This comes as a shock to TRACI.

Ring a bell?

TRACI. He's lying.

FITZ. Come on, Traci. That's beneath you.

Silence.

TRACI. Geoffrey . . . was an experiment.

FITZ. Highly inconclusive – judging by the number of times you repeated it. (*Pause.*) You're in love with him, aren't you?

TRACI. Don't be absurd.

FITZ. I mean Brito.

Pause.

TRACI. I have no sexual desire for him whatsoever.

FITZ. Rough trade only these days?

TRACI. Don't be unnecessarily offensive.

FITZ. I've no wish to be. But he's becoming intolerable. If you don't keep him in order . . . I'll tell him you and I used to screw each other senseless.

Pause.

TRACI. I'll speak to him – but I won't guarantee Brito's behaviour towards you or anyone else. And what you tell him is also beyond my control. But attempt to blackmail me again . . .

FITZ. And what?

Silence.

You'll kill me?

Pause.

TRACI. No. The sad fact is the only thing worth retrieving from this mess is our loyalty – to the king, and to one another.

FITZ. Always able to step back, aren't you? Onto the high ground.

Silence.

Why did you stop being my friend?

TRACI. I was getting married.

FITZ. That's not a reason.

TRACI. I thought it was.

FITZ. How's it been?

TRACI. I haven't made my wife unhappy. I love the children. I'd die for any one of them. That's how it's supposed to be, isn't it?

FITZ. Yes.

TRACI. Brito . . . is my infatuation with youth. My own youth, what remains of it. Do you understand?

FITZ. No.

TRACI. My last birthday I suddenly felt a lot closer to death than to life. Hit me really hard. A week later I become infatuated with a young man. The mechanics are so pathetically obvious – but . . . powerful just the same.

FITZ. And he has no idea, has he?

TRACI. No.

Silence.

Thing is it's not the looks. I do find him quite beautiful – but that's not it.

FITZ. Then what?

TRACI. The fearlessness. And the honesty. The ability to be utterly himself at every moment.

FITZ. You mean he's brainless, superficial and absurdly over-confident.

TRACI. Perhaps.

FITZ. Well . . . I won't tell him, Traci . . . because when it comes down to it I'm not a spiteful man – I'm much more unpleasant than that. (*Pause.*) I could fuck Brito and then cut his throat. Believe me.

Silence.

TRACI. I'm sorry if I made you unhappy.

FITZ. I spent the few years I could've spent making my son happy being miserable because of you. And then he died. And that's when I needed your *friendship*.

Silence.

But not a word. Nothing.

Silence.

There's a wonderful little irony about this place. The housekeeper's boy, he looks exactly like my son.

TRACI. Yes. That is ironic.

FITZ. The same age. If he'd lived.

Silence.

TRACI. I did . . . miss you.

FITZ. But not as much as I missed you. And that's the difference, isn't it? I needed you more than you needed me. And nothing can change that. (*Pause.*) Can it?

Pause.

TRACI. No.

Scene Four

Late the same night. The only light source is the fire.

BRITO *enters through the archway, nursing his swollen jaw and in a state of mild shock which makes him rather childlike. He pours some wine and takes a careful sip. He sits down.*

CATHERINE *enters by the door, carrying some firewood. She hesitates when she sees* BRITO *but then carries on, ignoring him. She stoops and tends the fire for a few moments.* BRITO *watches her every move. She turns and begins to leave the room.*

BRITO. I thought . . .

She ignores him and keeps walking towards the door.

Catherine!

CATHERINE *stops and turns towards him. His speech is distorted by the swelling.*

I thought you were magnificent this evening.

She says nothing, staring at him.

Magnificent.

He grins. CATHERINE *turns and walks towards the door.*

Catherine.

CATHERINE *stops and turns towards him.*

I want you to know I'm grateful.

Silence.

CATHERINE. How is it?

A brief silence.

BRITO. Why don't you have a look?

CATHERINE. Has the pain got worse?

BRITO. No.

CATHERINE. Then there's no point in looking.

Brief silence. She turns to go.

BRITO. Why are you up so late?

CATHERINE. I have work to do.

She turns to go.

BRITO. Can I ask you a question?

CATHERINE. If you must.

BRITO. Why do you despise us?

CATHERINE. You're serious?

BRITO. Yes. Tell me.

CATHERINE. Because you murdered a servant of God.

BRITO. All we did was try to carry out the orders of our king. We did what we did because loyalty demanded it.

CATHERINE. A King who gives orders to kill someone like that is a tyrant and doesn't deserve loyalty.

BRITO. Loyalty – once given – never asks questions. I'd follow Traci to the gates of Hell. And if he said 'Go in there and piss on their fires' I wouldn't say a word. I'd just have a big drink – and take out my dick.

CATHERINE. Men. You're just lazy. Anything to make life simple.

CATHERINE turns away and walks to the door.

BRITO. Can I say something else?

She stops and turns to him.

CATHERINE. If you wish, my lord.

BRITO. First of all I'm not a lord – not in the sense that the others are. I don't have a title or land.

BRITO moves towards her. He stops a few feet away.

BRITO. The other thing I wanted to say is . . . I've lusted after you from the moment I first saw you.

CATHERINE. I had no idea.

BRITO. I tried hard to hide it. But what I want to say is . . . now . . . I feel only admiration. And respect.

CATHERINE. Lust has been replaced by admiration and respect? Really?

BRITO. Well. Alright. Admiration tinged with . . . highly respectful lust. (*Pause.*) Nothing changes the fact that you're beautiful.

A pause.

CATHERINE. I hope you get some sleep.

CATHERINE turns away.

BRITO. Why are you alone?

She stops and turns.

CATHERINE. I'm not alone. I have my little boy.

BRITO. But no husband.

CATHERINE. I'm a widow.

BRITO. I know. But why haven't you remarried? And don't tell me no-one has wanted you.

CATHERINE. No-one suitable.

BRITO. What's suitable?

CATHERINE. Someone who has no children and can give my son more land, not take from him what he already has.

BRITO. Anything else?

CATHERINE. Yes. Someone I at least like and have respect for. (*Pause.*) It's not a combination I'm likely to find.

BRITO. So . . . life as a widow?

CATHERINE. Perhaps.

BRITO. But . . . you're not cold, by nature, are you?

CATHERINE. No.

BRITO. And yet you don't . . . have a lover?

CATHERINE. No.

BRITO. Have you never had one since your husband?

CATHERINE. No.

BRITO. Celibacy for someone like you is a sacrifice. One I understand.

CATHERINE. Really?

BRITO. Yes. I understand it to be utterly impossible. Otherwise I'd probably be in the church.

CATHERINE. Celibacy needn't stop you. They say our priest fucks anything from goats to little boys.

BRITO *is slightly taken aback, then amused.*

BRITO. He likes kids.

He grins. She's stony-faced.

Sorry. That's not at all funny, is it?

CATHERINE. No. (*Pause.*) Does Fitzherbert?

BRITO. What?

CATHERINE. Like kids. (*Pause.*) I've seen him . . . looking at my son.

Pause.

BRITO. No. The boy's safe. Believe me.

BRITO *winces and raises a hand to his cheek.*

CATHERINE. Is the pain getting worse?

BRITO. Yes.

CATHERINE. Do you want me to have a look at it?

BRITO. Yes. Please.

She walks past him to the table and the candles.

CATHERINE. Come over here by the light.

He moves over to her. She moves him towards the light.

Open your mouth.

CATHERINE *peers up into his mouth but has difficulty seeing clearly. She picks up the candles, takes his and gently adjusts the angle of his head.*

It's still very swollen but . . . it doesn't look angry.

BRITO. It's not infected?

CATHERINE. I don't think so.

She makes a move to turn away.

BRITO. Don't go.

There's a long silence while they look at each other. Then very slowly BRITO, *still holding one hand to his cheek, raises the other to her face, but without touching her.* CATHERINE *stands perfectly still, looking at him. She puts down the candles. Very gently the hand makes contact with her cheek. She closes her eyes as the hand caresses her face. After several moments* CATHERINE *suddenly opens her eyes, stares at him for a second then takes his face in both hands, gently at first and then with increasing pressure.* BRITO *winces and gasps, taking his hand from her cheek.*

CATHERINE. No . . . No!

CATHERINE *turns away and goes out, leaving* BRITO *gazing after her, holding his face and groaning. After a few moments he lets his hands fall to his sides.*

Scene Five

March 1171.

Early evening. The fire is giving off much more light. TRACI *and* BRITO *are cleaning and sharpening their weaponry – a process which fills this scene with business. They break off occasionally but the caress of carborundum on steel sounds throughout the scene.*

BRITO. Henry's smartest move ever was marrying Eleanor.

TRACI. It was his luckiest move. She chose him.

BRITO. What a woman. First time I saw her I was on one bank of the Loire and she was on the other. I thought Christ alive who is *that*? Amazing thing how you can fancy a woman at two hundred paces. Pathetic, really. She's a speck in the distance, she's that big, but you feel . . . *desire.*

BRITO *stands up.*

BRITO. When I was younger I used to get hard-ons that lasted for days. I did so much wanking I became ambidextrous just to keep up. I'd frig myself stupid but minutes later there it was again. Every morning there it was. Waiting. This thing (*Points at his crotch.*) is a fucking tyrant. A gross imposition. I mean there's so much more to life. There's so much to experience and understand. So much beauty and glory. But there's no idea so exciting, no emotion so uplifting, no place so beautiful that I wouldn't rather be up to my neck in shit so long as this thing was in a woman. Almost *any* woman.

TRACI. Well she'd better be tall.

BRITO. What? Oh yes! Otherwise . . . Yes.

Brief silence.

BRITO. It would just be nice to have, say, three months of every year erection-free. Just to be able to think about something else, and see the world with . . . clarity.

TRACI. You're a bit of an intellectual at heart aren't you?

BRITO. I am. I enjoyed studying – up to a point.

TRACI. You could've been a scholar.

BRITO. I could. I could've been so different. So much more *intelligent.*

They stop talking for a while. There's just the noise of steel being sharpened. Then BRITO *gets to his feet and sheaths his sword.*

I want to tell you something.

He draws his sword and shadow fights across the stage.

TRACI. Well?

BRITO *stops abruptly and turns to* TRACI.

BRITO. I'm in love.

TRACI. With whom?

BRITO. Catherine of course.

TRACI. Of course.

BRITO. She won't come near me but I adore her. For two months now – since she pulled my tooth. Now *this* isn't lust. I'm really in love with her.

TRACI. Love *is* lust – with temporary insanity thrown in.

BRITO. How many times have you been in love?

TRACI. Not often.

BRITO. How often?

TRACI. Four times.

BRITO. I fall in love at least twice a year. Not only do I have this tyrant to put up with, I have to fall in love, too. And always with women who don't want it. And then there's all that wanting, that *joy* just . . . a fingertip away.

CATHERINE *enters by the door. She is soaking wet and chilled to the bone, shaking, racked with cold. She moves across the room in a fevered trance, giving no sign of being aware of* BRITO *and* TRACI, *and stands in front of the fire, trembling.* BRITO *and* TRACI *are speechless.* TRACI *gets to his feet and smiles.*

TRACI. I think I'll let you deal with this.

TRACI *picks up the weaponry and exits through the arch.*

BRITO. Catherine . . .

BRITO approaches her.

Catherine. You're soaking wet.

CATHERINE gives no sign of being aware of his presence. She just goes on shaking and staring at the fire. He reaches out and touches her.

My God. You're frozen. What's happened to you? Catherine!

He takes her by the shoulders.

Catherine! What's happened to you?

She looks as though she might be trying to speak, but can't.

You've got to get those clothes off.

BRITO exits through the arch and reappears with a blanket.

You've got to get those clothes off. Catherine!

She's unresponsive. He's at a loss for a moment then holds out the blanket to her.

Take the blanket. I'll leave you while you undress.

No response. BRITO decides to act. He drops the blanket, takes her jacket from her shoulders and drops it. He pauses, waiting for a protest, before he begins to unbutton the back of her dress. He pulls it open, exposing her shoulders. He's momentarily stopped by the sight of her bare back and then begins slowly to pull the dress down to her waist. He pauses again, overwhelmed by the sight of her body. Suddenly he picks up the blanket and wraps it round her, clasping it with one hand at her neck.

Hold it!

No reaction. He lifts one of her hands to her neck.

Hold it!

CATHERINE grips the blanket. BRITO gets down on his knees, puts his hands under the blanket and pulls her dress down.

Lift your foot.

She lifts one foot.

And the other one.

BRITO *pulls the dress out from under the blanket. He stands and looks at her.*

What's happened to you?

No response. BRITO *takes the blanket from her hand and wraps it round her so it's tucked and held around her shoulders. He turns and throws some wood on the fire, grabs a pair of bellows and pumps furiously for several seconds, then turns* CATHERINE *so her back is to the fire.* CATHERINE *gives a great sigh and takes several long, deep breaths.*

CATHERINE. They didn't kill me. I'm alive. I'm alive.

BRITO. What happened?

She stares at him, feeling the heat soaking into her back. He's overwhelmed by the intensity of her gaze. CATHERINE, *radiant with joy, clasps him around the neck, letting the blanket fall away.*

CATHERINE. I'm alive!

CATHERINE *kisses him with an aggression that makes him draw back, shocked, before he responds. They kiss passionately.* BRITO *suddenly breaks off, picks up the blanket and very tenderly wraps it around her. He picks her up and carries her out through the arch.*

Scene Six

An hour later. There's the sound of MORVILLE's *desperate voice from outside the room: 'Kate! Kate!' A pause and then 'Kate! Kate!'*

MORVILLE *enters through the door in a state of near-panic.*

MORVILLE. Kate!

BRITO *appears in the archway.* TRACI *appears alongside him.*

Where's Catherine?

BRITO *hesitates, waiting for* TRACI.

MORVILLE. Have you seen Catherine?

TRACI. Yes.

MORVILLE. Recently?

BRITO. Yes.

MORVILLE. How recent?

TRACI. About an hour.

MORVILLE. Thank God! (*Pause.*) Was she alright?

BRITO. She was soaking wet. Apart from that, fine. She's gone to bed.

MORVILLE. Did she say anything?

BRITO. Just that she was cold.

TRACI. What happened?

MORVILLE. They accused her of witchcraft! They made her walk out on the ice over one of the trout pools. She went through and straight down. And stayed down! The bastards probably weighted her. *Minutes later* one of the trout farmers said they should get her out in case she poisoned the fish! Otherwise she'd still be down there! They laid her out dead as a stone. Then she opened her eyes and stood up! There's pandemonium! They're running around screaming about miracles and divine retribution. Stupid, ignorant pigs!

Silence.

Where's Fitz?

TRACI. In bed with one of his guards.

MORVILLE. Christ . . . !

BRITO. Excuse me. I know it's early but I didn't sleep at all last night and . . . I'm going to bed. (*Pause.*) So. Goodnight.

TRACI. Goodnight.

MORVILLE. Goodnight. Sleep well.

BRITO. Thank you. I'll try.

BRITO *exits through the arch.* MORVILLE *moves towards the door.*

MORVILLE. I'm going to check the guard.

TRACI. It's been done. We should all get some sleep. And we'll talk to Catherine in the morning.

MORVILLE. Yes. You're right.

MORVILLE heads towards the arch. TRACI follows.

Things are getting out of hand, Traci.

They exit. After a few moments, CATHERINE appears in the arch. She's wearing the same dress – no longer soaking but still very damp. She hesitates briefly, checking the room is clear, then enters. She's followed by BRITO. He catches hold of her shoulder, turning her to him.

CATHERINE. I have to go. (*Pause.*) Promise me you won't tell anyone.

BRITO. I give you my word.

CATHERINE. Thank you.

BRITO embraces her. She's distant.

BRITO. What's the matter? (*Pause.*) What's the matter?

CATHERINE. I shouldn't have done it.

BRITO. Are you serious?

CATHERINE. Yes.

There's an edge of panic and fear in BRITO's voice.

BRITO. I don't believe you.

CATHERINE. I shouldn't have done it! I wouldn't have if . . . I'd known what I was doing.

BRITO. You did know what you were doing. Believe me.

CATHERINE. I wasn't normal. I'd nearly died.

BRITO. To come to life again. With the warmth of my body!

BRITO kisses her. CATHERINE doesn't respond.

CATHERINE. This isn't what I want.

BRITO. I want to marry you.

CATHERINE. You're in no position to marry anyone! And anyway . . . you'll have to leave here. And I can't go with you. Everything we have – my son and me – everything we

have is here. (*Pause.*) There's nothing can come of this –
whether I'm in love with you or not. It has to stop.

BRITO. Why? Why can't we be lovers?

CATHERINE. No!

BRITO. Why not?

CATHERINE. Because . . .

BRITO. Tell me!

CATHERINE. I want . . . something else. (*Pause.*) Someone
else.

BRITO. Someone else? Here? In Knaresborough?

CATHERINE. Yes.

He thinks for a moment.

BRITO. Morville! Morville?

Silence.

CATHERINE. Yes.

BRITO. Morville! But . . . his situation's the same as mine.

CATHERINE. No. Whether he's here or in Palestine, he has
land and it's here. He's a good man who will learn to love
my son and . . . what he has is here! In a place and amongst
people I know.

BRITO. People who tried to kill you.

CATHERINE. Only some of them. The priest and his
followers.

BRITO. They're all mad around here. You can't live amongst
people like these.

CATHERINE. Yes, I can. I can make a good life for my son –
and for me. I won't let anything get in the way of that. I
won't.

Silence.

BRITO. Are you in love with me?

A long pause.

I'm in love with you.

A long pause.

And you're in love with me. I know you are. (*Pause.*) What happened in there was wonderful. (*Pause.*) Wasn't it?

A long pause.

Tell me. Just tell me, just say it. It was wonderful.

CATHERINE. It was wonderful.

CATHERINE *moves forward and puts her arms around him. They are like this for a long time. They kiss.*

BRITO. You love me. Tell me you love me.

CATHERINE. I want you to tear me apart – and eat every piece of me.

BRITO. Then let me! You can have Morville later.

CATHERINE *breaks away.*

CATHERINE. No. No! If he found out – and he would find out – I'd be worthless to him. And, anyway . . . I have to offer him all of me. (*Pause.*) All of what's left of me.

CATHERINE *turns away and walks quickly to the door.*

BRITO. I'm in love with you, Catherine.

She pauses at the door.

CATHERINE. I won't allow it to happen. Believe me. I won't.

BRITO. I've been in love with you for weeks. Then that in there happens, the most wonderful experience of my life. And . . . you tell me it means nothing. Nothing has changed. You *bitch!* You cold, cold bitch!

CATHERINE. That's better.

BRITO. Oh is it? I'll tell him. I'll tell him you fucked like a dream – when all I wanted was just . . . to hold you. To adore you. To care for you.

She looks at him for a few moments.

CATHERINE. No. You won't.

BRITO. How can you be so sure?

CATHERINE. Because you're too sweet natured.

BRITO. What makes you think that?

CATHERINE. I know. I've been to bed with you.

BRITO. He doesn't deserve you. Christ if he were a better man than me in any way maybe I could begin to bear it! I hate him. Catherine, I'll kill him!

CATHERINE smiles at him for a moment, then turns and leaves. BRITO stares after her. He starts to shake his head and walk aimlessly, desperately about the room.

Oh sweet Christ! Help me!

TRACI enters by the archway. He's carrying two sets of armour and weaponry.

Traci. Tell me. What's going to happen to us?

TRACI. Tonight? Or in general?

BRITO. In general.

They begin the process of arming themselves. Occasionally, BRITO breaks off to shadow fight.

TRACI. What happens in the end is between Henry and the Pope. The Pope will impose the penance he's agreed with Henry. Meanwhile every day that passes people will care a little less until they no longer care enough to take us on. Then we can leave. For Rome. That may be weeks from now, maybe months.

BRITO. Months. Fuck. If I haven't killed Fitz in that time, it'll be a miracle.

TRACI. You seriously underestimate him.

BRITO. I could handle Fitz.

BRITO mimes a swift killing.

TRACI. No. You couldn't.

BRITO. What are you saying? Fitz!?

TRACI. Yes! Fitz! What you're going to learn out there tonight Fitz learnt years ago many times over. It makes a difference!

BRITO. So why am I here and not Fitz?

TRACI. He's too slow and too unfit to take on numbers. But one to one he'd still be too much for you believe me.

BRITO *is shocked and humbled.*

Ten years ago Fitz was the most formidable fighter I'd ever seen.

BRITO. Better than you?

TRACI. Better than me.

Pause.

Underestimating Fitz was the biggest mistake of our lives.

BRITO. What do you mean?

TRACI. When we found Becket in the cathedral what we wanted – you, me, Morville – was to arrest him and deliver him to Henry. Becket stood his ground. What happened next?

BRITO. You said 'Take him'. We grabbed him, tried to lift him up to carry him out. He put up a fight, the place was filling up for evensong, we made a decision under pressure: leave without a result or kill him. We killed him.

TRACI. No. *We* didn't kill him.

TRACI *mimes the actions.*

Morville's keeping the public at bay. You and I get hold of Becket. There are two monks attending him. One runs and the other stays. Becket's stronger than we think. The monk's hanging on to him. Becket gets loose. He spins round like this. Fitz is coming at him. And bang – Becket catches Fitz with his elbow and Fitz goes down. You and I aren't looking at Fitz, we're trying to get hold of Becket. Then Fitz is up. I look at him. He's looking at Becket. Not angry. This isn't a man losing his head. Dead still. Dead calm. I remember because what he did next came as a surprise. He went for him. Fitz' sword is coming down like this onto Becket's head. The monk puts his arm up. The sword smashes his arm, comes off it and into Becket's neck. Becket goes to his knees and crosses himself. And he knows, we all know, he's a dead man. And I'm transfixed with horror and fear. But *he* – Becket . . . smiles at me. A look of *triumph*. Because he'd got what he wanted. Martyrdom! And I saw

the monstrous vanity of the man! That's when I struck him.
And you came in behind me.

BRITO. Yes, off his head, straight onto the deck and smashed
my best sword in two. Fuck that still pisses me off.

TRACI. The point is, Brito, what happened was between
Fitz and Becket. All we did is take part. Fitz killed him.
The question is why? Because Henry gave him separate
instructions? Or did he have his own reasons?

BRITO *stares at* TRACI. *He's incredulous.*

BRITO. We should kill him.

TRACI. It's irrelevant. Killing Fitz now changes nothing.
Unless you have something to gain, revenge is for
simpletons! Always remember that.

BRITO *is confused by* TRACI's *dismissive tone.*

Forget it. And say nothing. Fitz will tell us himself sooner
or later.

BRITO. Why?

TRACI. Duplicity isn't his style. Fitz is a very honest man.

BRITO. Fuck. Now you have lost me.

TRACI. Me too. I don't believe a word I'm saying. And I
believe every word.

BRITO. I know what you mean. Doubt. Ambivalence. Always
been a problem of mine. Don't know why. My father was
very decisive. Wrong every fucking time. But at least he
enjoyed a sense of conviction.

BRITO *goes into a whirling sword exercise. He stops and
offers the sword to* TRACI.

Try it.

TRACI *takes the sword and goes into an exercise.*

Good isn't it? The other one was even better.

TRACI. Nice weight. Where was this made?

BRITO. Austria. My father mortgaged his estate to upgrade his
armour then had a stroke. Now he's just the tenant and I've
got the armour.

TRACI *hands the sword to* BRITO.

How many do you think there'll be?

TRACI. No more than a dozen. The ringleaders.

BRITO. Well trained?

TRACI. No.

BRITO. Well armed?

TRACI. Not unless they're expecting us. Ready?

BRITO. I don't know.

TRACI. Brito. This isn't a tournament we're going to.

BRITO. All I can think about is Catherine.

TRACI. Her life depends on how good you are tonight. Think about that. And tell me you're ready.

He thinks.

BRITO. I'm ready. You?

TRACI. Yes. (*Pause.*) Are you frightened?

BRITO. Yes. A little.

TRACI. Good. So am I. A little fear is good.

BRITO. I'm ready.

They look at each other for a moment. BRITO *spontaneously moves forward and they embrace. They part and* BRITO *looks at* TRACI *for a moment.*

Do you like me, Traci?

TRACI. Of course.

BRITO. Do you like me as much as I like you?

TRACI. Hard to say.

BRITO. Do you need me as much as I need you?

TRACI. This isn't the time.

BRITO. Oh yes it is. An hour from now one or both of us could be dead. She won't tell me she loves me. But you. The man I admire above all others. Before I go out there and die with you I want you to tell me you love me.

A long pause.

TRACI. I love you.

Pause.

BRITO. Kiss me.

TRACI. Brito . . .

BRITO. Go on. Kiss me. Just kiss me.

BRITO *kisses* TRACI *quickly, firmly, on the mouth.* TRACI *is totally unresponsive, barely moving.*

You love me. And I love you.

TRACI. Good. Now. Listen to me. Don't think about anything else, just listen to me.

They establish a moment of communion.

Stay close to me. And remember two things. Only a few will really count, the rest will be terrified. Don't waste time on them. Pick out the ones that are least frightened and disable them. Legs. Throat. Quickly. Quickly as you can. Put them down. Make them safe. Don't worry about killing them. We can do that later. The second thing is . . . the thrill of battle is more dangerous than the horror. Don't start enjoying it. If you're enjoying it you're wasting time – time enough for someone to kill you. And if one of us is down the other is probably finished, too. (*Pause.*) Stay close to me, Brito.

They put their helmets on then go quietly to the door. They exit.

ACT TWO

Scene One

The early hours of the next morning. The stage is almost dark except for light coming from the stairs door. Two barely discernible figures are on stage, still and waiting. The door opens and two more figures, equally obscure, back through the door with caution and difficulty.

VOICE (*whispers*). Leave him in the cold. He won't bleed so much.

They straighten up, turn and creep conspiratorially to centre stage. One of the stationary figures bends into the fireplace and lights a taper. The two central figures freeze as two candles are lit. BRITO *and* TRACI *have been caught red-handed by* MORVILLE *and* FITZ.

FITZ. What the holy fuck have you two been doing?

FITZ lights more candles.

BRITO. We went out.

MORVILLE. Out! Where?

TRACI. Not far. Just for a stroll.

MORVILLE: Outside the castle?

TRACI. Yes.

MORVILLE. Why are you armed?

MORVILLE has been drawn forward to BRITO *and* TRACI, *intrigued by something. He looks closely at them both. He's appalled. He turns to* FITZ.

They're covered in blood. (*To* TRACI.) You're covered in blood!

FITZ lights more candles. TRACI *and* BRITO *turn and examine each other. They, too, are surprised.*

TRACI. You've got a nasty cut somewhere, Brito!

BRITO. Nosebleed.

MORVILLE. It looks as if you've spent the night in a slaughterhouse!

BRITO goes to the side table and pours wine into two cups. He picks them up and pauses.

BRITO. Oh, sorry. Anybody else?

MORVILLE. No! . . . Thank you.

BRITO smiles at MORVILLE's politeness and walks towards to him, handing one of the cups to TRACI as he does so. He stands in front of MORVILLE, smiling radiantly at him. He's on the high of a lifetime.

BRITO. Morv' you are such a, such a sweet man. I love you. I mean it. You are so adorable. Kiss me, Morv'. Kiss me.

BRITO suddenly puts an arm around MORVILLE and tries to kiss him on the mouth. MORVILLE recoils and pushes BRITO off.

Why will no-one kiss me? Traci's the same. He won't kiss me.

MORVILLE wipes his face and looks at his hands.

MORVILLE. Whose blood is this?

TRACI. Ours.

FITZ picks up a sword and thrusts it between BRITO's legs.

FITZ. Tell me whose blood it is or I'll ruin you.

Everyone is quiet. They know he means it.

TRACI. Tell him.

BRITO. This is how it happened. You two have gone to bed, right? Me and Brainy are drinking. And then – get this if you fucking please! – Traci tells me I'm no good in the field. Too impulsive. I said get your kit on. It's you and me outside. Now.

FITZ raises the sword. BRITO slowly goes up on tiptoe.

We did get a bit carried away. Lucky neither of us was badly hurt, really.

FITZ. You – !

MORVILLE. Fitz! Wait!

MORVILLE steps up to TRACI *and takes something from a fold in* TRACI'*s collar. He turns to* BRITO.

If the blood's yours then whose is this?

MORVILLE holds up something between his thumb and index finger.

BRITO. Whose is what?

MORVILLE. This!

FITZ. What is it?

MORVILLE. It's someone's *ear*!

Another pause. BRITO *raises each hand in turn to his ears.*

BRITO. It's not mine. Is it yours Traci?

TRACI *starts to chuckle, shaking his head.*

It's not his. Oh dear, dear, dear – someone's missing an ear. (*Pause.*) Could it be our guest?

TRACI. Could be.

FITZ. Who are you talking about?

BRITO. We asked someone back for a chat.

FITZ. Who?

BRITO. Dunno. I think he's died on us.

MORVILLE. Died?

TRACI. The stairs were too much for him.

MORVILLE. What stairs?

BRITO. Those out there.

FITZ lowers his sword and goes to the door. He opens it. A body slumps into the room.

MORVILLE. My god. My god . . .

MORVILLE goes to the door.

My god. What have you done? You madmen. You madmen . . .

BRITO. Yes, yes – but is it his?

MORVILLE *stares at* BRITO, *speechless, still taking in the implications of what he's seen.*

TRACI. Pull yourself together Morville! The ear! Is it his?

MORVILLE, *as in a trance, turns and looks. He turns back into the room and nods.*

BRITO. Well don't look so upset. He's not going to miss it now is he?

MORVILLE *drops the ear onto the table.*

FITZ. Who is he?

MORVILLE. Peter Wigmore.

FITZ. Yes?

MORVILLE. Local farmer, magistrate and leader of the county council.

FITZ. You're not serious.

MORVILLE. Yes. Probably the most influential man in the area.

TRACI. Was. Now he's one of the least influential. Wouldn't you say that, Brito?

BRITO. Let's ask him.

BRITO *goes to the door and drags the corpse into the room.* BRITO *props it up against the table leg. He takes off his sword and props it up next to the corpse. He picks up the ear from the table and holds it to his mouth.*

Oi! Are you influential?

BRITO *gives the corpse a kick.*

I don't see a lot of influence there, Morville.

MORVILLE. Like Becket you mean? He's dead so he can't hurt us? You imbeciles! Half the county will be up in arms against us.

TRACI. No they won't. No-one saw us.

FITZ. How did you leave?

TRACI. The sallyport of course. No-one saw us – going out or coming in. Except the guards.

MORVILLE. What about out there?

TRACI. No-one saw us.

MORVILLE. There'll be a mob at our gates by morning.

TRACI. Dear, dear, Brito – the simplicity of the average mind. While he and his brothers and their followers were alive –

MORVILLE. *Were* alive . . . !?

   MORVILLE *is stunned.*

   He and his brothers . . . and their followers . . .

   MORVILLE *looks at* FITZ *as if looking for help to comprehend.*

   . . . and his brothers . . . and their followers . . . ? You've killed others?

TRACI. Of course. Plus three dogs and a couple of horses. Slaughter-house was right. Brito went berserk.

MORVILLE. How many?

TRACI (*to* BRITO). What do you think?

BRITO. Well . . . there were two at the gatehouse, and three outside the house weren't there? Or was it four?

TRACI. Three to start with but someone came out. So yes we killed seven outside.

BRITO. Then we got back on our horses and rode into the house. Should've seen their faces. 'Who the fuck are these two!?' It was perfect. We're not talking surprise. Just total incomprehension. 'Who the fuck are these two lunatics!'

TRACI. Touching isn't it? Gets so excited when you take him out. How *many,* Brito?

BRITO. Well I see nine men around that table as we ride in.

MORVILLE. You killed them *all*?

BRITO. Of course. I mean, thing about killing people is once you start you want to finish don't you? It was easy. In fact it was great. We must do it again soon, Traci. And there were the three hiding in the cellar.

MORVILLE. No. Dear God. Tell me you're not serious. Tell me this is just a horrible, terrible joke.

BRITO. So that's . . .

MORVILLE. Nineteen . . . You've killed nineteen people tonight!

BRITO (*pointing at* WIGMORE). Twenty.

TRACI. Should only have been nineteen of course.

FITZ. Only nineteen . . .

TRACI. For the time being. Unfortunately he put up a good fight. Couldn't understand we didn't want to kill him only wanted a chat. Pity. I did want him to explain to you what they were up to.

MORVILLE. Twenty. Women? Children?

TRACI. Of course not. What's the point?

FITZ. In this case to eliminate witnesses.

TRACI. We weren't displaying a coat of arms!

MORVILLE. Twenty people . . .

TRACI. You have to understand we were in serious danger from this ambitious farmer! The first rule of power is to turn your enemies into friends. You can only do that if your enemies think you have something to offer. What have we to offer the people here? The second rule of power is if you can't turn your enemies into friends you must lay them waste. Destroy them. Protect the weak, love your own, *destroy* your enemies.

MORVILLE. We're still king's men! Henry's orders were to seek penitent obscurity while diplomacy takes its course. He said absolutely nothing about wiping out half of West Yorkshire!

TRACI. Henry would understand.

FITZ. *Henry* has built an empire without a single major engagement and with the loss of no more than a handful of lives in 16 years while out-manouevring the greatest powers in Europe! You've killed twenty in one night in fucking *Knaresborough!*

MORVILLE. Henry believes he's created a new era in which power is about diplomacy not war.

TRACI. That day will never come. There's no possibility of diplomacy with men who have no fear of death – either because they're mad – like Becket – or because they think *they* are going to do the killing. Like him.

BRITO. Exactly. Brainy's right. We've removed the immediate threat by force. *Now* we get diplomatic. We put up a banner on the tower. A big one. It says 'Very sorry we killed the Wigmores everybody – but so long as you behave yourself, we won't fucking kill *you!*'

WIGMORE *opens his eyes and is on his feet in an instant. He takes hold of* BRITO *from behind and puts a knife to his throat. The others freeze.* BRITO *grins, raises a hand and counts them – one, two, three, and himself.*

That you, Wigmore?

WIGMORE. Blink and I'll kill you.

TRACI. Kill him and we'll kill you.

WIGMORE. I am surprised.

TRACI. Spare him and we'll spare you.

WIGMORE. Now I'm incredulous.

TRACI. You have my word.

WIGMORE. I want my freedom.

FITZ *laughs derisively.*

TRACI. Spare him and you have it.

MORVILLE. You'll be freed, Wigmore, I give you my word.

WIGMORE (*indicating* FITZ). I want his word.

MORVILLE. *My* word is what matters here, Wigmore! Release him.

WIGMORE (*to* FITZ). You! Come over here and kiss my foot.

Brief silence.

FITZ. Fuck off, eat shit and die.

WIGMORE. Kiss my foot now or *he* dies. In five seconds. (*Pause.*) One, two, three –

TRACI *smashes the handle of his sword into the side of* FITZ*'s head, poleaxing him.*

TRACI. We're unanimous now, Wigmore.

> WIGMORE *still hesitates.* TRACI *drags* FITZ *across the floor so that* FITZ's *head lies on* WIGMORE's *feet.*

Release my friend.

> WIGMORE *releases* BRITO.

Good. Now let's have a drink. Sit down.

> WIGMORE *sits at the table.* MORVILLE *stoops to check* FITZ.

MORVILLE (*worried*). You hit him hard, Traci.

BRITO. Good.

> BRITO *kicks* FITZ *in the back.*

TRACI. Leave him!

> MORVILLE *stands and pours himself a drink of wine.* BRITO *picks up the ear from the table and offers it to* WIGMORE.

BRITO. I think this belongs to you.

> WIGMORE *takes the ear.*

WIGMORE. Not much use to me now is it?

> WIGMORE *throws the ear into the fire.* BRITO *pours some wine and puts it in front of* WIGMORE.

BRITO. Here. You feel bad now – drink that.

> WIGMORE *drinks.*

WIGMORE. Christ!

BRITO. My apologies.

TRACI. Peter. I'm going to explain to Morville why Brito and I felt it necessary to do what we've done tonight. You and your brothers were plotting rebellion on the pretext that this castle is occupied by Satanic powers – but with the purpose of acquiring the castle and Morville's rights.

WIGMORE. Yes.

MORVILLE. Peter! Your father and mine were friends!

WIGMORE. Your father had no friends.

MORVILLE. That's not true.

TRACI. It doesn't matter Morville! What matters is that tonight Wigmore gathered his brothers and conspirators together to organise stage two of an insurrection. Stage one was carried out yesterday afternoon with the seizure of Catherine at his instigation in collusion with the local priest. Something to test local mood and opinion. Something to get the mob fired up for the big day. Am I right, Wigmore?

WIGMORE. Yes.

TRACI (*to* MORVILLE). You see? This man has intelligence. (*Pause.*) It's very simple, Morville. They would've killed us all. Including the boy.

CATHERINE *enters, half-asleep, wearing a white night-dress. She stares at* WIGMORE. WIGMORE *struggles to his feet in a paroxysm of terror.*

WIGMORE. Forgive me. Please. Catherine. Forgive me.

WIGMORE *starts to choke and fit.*

Forgive me. In the name of the blessed Virgin . . . the merciful Christ . . .

BRITO. What's the matter with him?

WIGMORE. Forgive me . . . Catherine . . .

WIGMORE *collapses.* MORVILLE *feels for a pulse.*

TRACI. Is he dead?

MORVILLE. I think so. What happened?

TRACI. He died of fear. Which is odd given how much courage the man has shown tonight.

BRITO. Fear? Fear of what?

TRACI *turns to* CATHERINE.

TRACI. Catherine. The risen maid of Knaresborough. The witch made saint.

Brief silence.

BRITO. Fucking hell! Eerier and eerier!

Brief silence.

FITZ. I can't move my legs.

FITZ is leaning back on his hands, staring at his legs. The others are shocked. It's the first time anyone has ever seen FITZ show fear.

I can't move my legs!

BRITO turns away, exultant.

BRITO. Yes! What a night! What a fucking *night!*

Scene Two

September.

CATHERINE enters through the arch, pulling a bathtub. She places it in front of the fire. She exits through the door, returning after a few seconds with a large bucket. She pours hot water from the bucket into the bathtub then exits through the door, returning to repeat the same process.

CATHERINE (*shouts*). It's ready!

MORVILLE, BRITO and TRACI enter. TRACI is carrying FITZ on his back. They're unclothed, covered only by large towels. MORVILLE helps TRACI lower FITZ into a chair. MORVILLE pours himself some wine, goes to the fireplace and stands with his back to the fire, his towel raised to expose his buttocks. The atmosphere is pleasant and relaxed.

BRITO. Who's first this week?

FITZ. I am.

BRITO. You sure?

FITZ. You were first last week. I was last. This week I'm first, you're second.

BRITO picks up a sword and approaches FITZ, playfully threatening.

BRITO. Would you care to re-think that one, Ugly?

FITZ. I'm first.

MORVILLE. He's right. He's first, you're second, I'm third, Traci's last.

CATHERINE *enters with another pan of water and begins pouring it into the bathtub.*

FITZ. Catherine, whose turn to be first?

CATHERINE. Yours.

BRITO. Okay. But if he pisses in my water I'm going to kill him.

FITZ. Half of me could still take one of you, Brito.

BRITO *and* TRACI *take hold of* FITZ *and gently lift him out of the chair.*

BRITO. He's getting heavier.

They carry FITZ *to the tub and slowly lower him into it. He leans back and makes himself comfortable.*

FITZ. Ahhh . . . Fantastic. (*Pause.*) Nurse! The ladle.

TRACI *picks up a large ladle. He starts to pour water over* FITZ.

Aaah. Fantastic.

TRACI *continues to ladle water over* FITZ.

Enough, thank you, nurse.

TRACI *stops.*

BRITO. That water looks greeny-yellow to me already.

FITZ. My bladder control's improving – but it's not perfect, Brito.

BRITO. Git.

FITZ. Oh my god how full of simple delights is this world! Who needs anything more than this? Devoted companions, a warm room, a hot bath – and a chance to piss all over Brito.

TRACI. There's one thing we need if we're here much longer. Money.

BRITO. Fucking right! The town tarts are demanding cash! And local coin at that.

FITZ. Fucking nerve. They should be paying us. I've never seen a more gruesome bunch.

BRITO. Yes, but . . . that Margaret. The big blonde with the warts. I'm really getting to like her! (*Pause.*) Amazing what you'll get used to, isn't it? Six months ago I thought I'd go out of my mind if I spent another week in this place. Now here I am about to take a bath topped up with other people's urine and I feel . . . not too bad.

A pause.

TRACI. We could open to the public.

BRITO. Do what?

TRACI. Open to the public.

MORVILLE. We can't do that!

TRACI. There's no reason why not, managed properly.

BRITO. Be nice to see some new faces.

A pause as they all think about it. Suddenly FITZ *heaves himself upright in the bath.*

FITZ. Traci! Come here. Quickly. Please!

TRACI goes over to the tub.

TRACI. What?

FITZ. Lift my left foot.

TRACI raises FITZ*'s foot.*

Yes! (*Pause.*) Rub the bottom of it!

TRACI. Can you feel it?

FITZ. Yes! Yes I can!

TRACI, delighted, starts to tickle the bottom of the foot. FITZ *stares at his toes.*

They're moving! My toes are moving!

They're transfixed by FITZ*'s toes as he concentrates every ounce of his being on moving them. After several seconds, the others start to turn away.*

Look!

They all focus on his foot again. Then, after several more seconds, the toes move. General delight.

They're moving! I'm regenerate! God is healing me! He forgives me! He forgives me! He forgives us all!!

Suddenly MORVILLE *is on his feet, yelling triumphantly.*

MORVILLE. Yes! Yes! Yes!!!

He stabs a finger towards the corner.

You see? God *knows!* He understands! *He* knows why we did it! He knows you were a monster of vanity, a grotesque obstruction to human progress! So you can fuck off . . . !!

MORVILLE *hurls his cup into the corner.* BRITO *snatches up a sword.*

BRITO. Where is he Morville? Tell me where he is and I'll deal with him.

MORVILLE. No. I'm the only one who didn't strike him. It has to be me.

MORVILLE *grabs* BRITO's *sword.*

It has to be me.

MORVILLE *rushes across the room, raising the sword to strike a powerful blow, and then stops, dead still.*

BRITO. Go on, Morville. Take him!

MORVILLE *is completely still for several seconds.*

Go *on*, Morville! Do it!

Very slowly, MORVILLE *lowers the sword and falls to his knees.*

MORVILLE. Forgive me. Forgive me. Forgive me. Forgive me.

TRACI *and* BRITO, *deeply moved, watch* MORVILLE. FITZ *watches all three, nodding to himself and smiling.*

TRACI. For eight months the madness was out there. Now it's in here. Now the madness is us.

Scene Three

Later the same night. The bathtub is still in position.
CATHERINE *enters carrying a basket of wood. She puts
the basket down and starts feeding the fire. After loading on
several logs she picks up the bellows and fans the fire. Then
she turns, takes hold of the bathtub and drags it towards the
door.*

*She stops, noticing a heavy coat hanging over a chair. She
picks it up and, holding it in both hands, breathes in its smell.
She slowly buries her face in it.*

MORVILLE *appears in the archway, wearing a coat over a
nightdress. He's holding a document which is rolled and
sealed. He watches* CATHERINE *as she holds the coat to her,
swaying gently, eyes closed.*

MORVILLE. What are you doing?

> CATHERINE *is startled. They look at each other for a
> second or two.*

Put it down. Please.

> CATHERINE *puts the coat back on the chair.* MORVILLE
> *puts the document on the table and walks towards her. She
> tenses, uncertain and a little afraid. He stops in front of her.
> She shivers.*

Are you cold?

CATHERINE: *Yes.*

> MORVILLE *holds open his coat and folds it around*
> CATHERINE, *gently holding her to him. Then she puts her
> arms around him. They are like this for a while.*
> MORVILLE *starts to weep.* CATHERINE *wipes the tears
> from his eyes, stroking his face and kissing him on his
> forehead and cheeks.*

Do you forgive me?

CATHERINE. Yes.

> *Silence. He draws away from her.*

MORVILLE. Go to bed, Kate.

CATHERINE *goes to the door.*

CATHERINE. Good night.

MORVILLE. Good night, Kate.

CATHERINE goes, shutting the door behind her.

MORVILLE *picks up the document, lights more candles, breaks the seal and starts to read. As he reads, his reactions alternate between anger and despair.*

No! . . . No! . . . Oh Christ no . . .

He sighs and hangs his head in utter despondency. Then he gathers himself and shouts towards the archway.

Traci! Brito!

He reads the letter again.

Traci! Brito!

BRITO *appears in the arch.*

BRITO. What?

TRACI *appears in the arch.*

TRACI. What's that?

MORVILLE. A letter from the king.

BRITO. What's he say?

MORVILLE. He's going to Pembroke.

BRITO. Where?

MORVILLE. Pembroke.

BRITO. What for?

MORVILLE. To organise an army for Ireland.

BRITO. Ireland! And us? Anything about us?

MORVILLE. We're to stay here until he returns.

BRITO. When will that be? He could be there for months.

MORVILLE. This says at least six.

BRITO. Six months!

MORVILLE. At least. Make that a year.

BRITO. Oh thanks for that, Morville. Why not make it two years and *really* cheer me up?

MORVILLE. And we're on our own. He says he's only been able to resist great pressure to punish us by saying punishment is the Pope's prerogative. He'll do what he can but essentially it's now between us and the Pope. We have to go to Rome and receive sentence. But we're to stay here until he returns from Ireland.

BRITO. Six more months. A year even! I can't face another winter here! Take me to your place in Devon, Traci. Get me out of here! Come on Traci. Let's just go.

TRACI. We wouldn't make Beverley let alone Exeter.

BRITO. Things have calmed down out there now.

MORVILLE. That's because no-one out there's clapped eyes on us for months. (*Pause.*) Things have gone unbelievably well for us here.

BRITO. Oh yes. I'm having a great time.

TRACI. He's right. They love us here now. In Catherine surviving the ordeal they've had a miracle. Divine intervention. And the most spectacular divine retribution against her accusers. A halfwit would guess it must have been us but they prefer to believe that Knaresborough currently commands God's undivided attention. It's all been most diverting for them and meanwhile, yes, they've calmed down a bit. And they've come to feel strangely flattered that the most notorious criminals in the world are resident in their midst. They feel excited and a little warmed by the aura of danger – so long as it comes at them through the bars of a cage. Presume to go riding about the county and see what happens. The good people of Yorkshire would regard that as serious provocation.

BRITO. But six months! Maybe a year!

MORVILLE *puts the letter down in front of* TRACI, *who picks it up and reads it.*

TRACI. You have to admire him. What a stroke. Brilliant, really.

BRITO. Who? What?

TRACI. Henry. He's gone to Ireland to get the Irish nobility back under control. His control. At the same time he'll sort out the Irish Bishops – and bring them back under the Vatican's control. He's expanding his empire and paying off his debt to the Pope at the same time. That's not an easy combination to achieve.

BRITO. For fuck's sake! It's a disaster! And you give it 'Oh how interesting! 'A' equals 'X' to the power of ten plus the cubed root of my *dick!*' (*Pause.*) Six months! A year!!

Silence.

TRACI. We should just be grateful we're spending it here and not in Ireland.

BRITO. I'd rather be fighting the Irish than stuck in this hole!

MORVILLE. Have you ever fought in Ireland?

BRITO. No.

MORVILLE. No. Nor has anyone else.

BRITO. What's that supposed to mean?

MORVILLE. It means no-one fights in Ireland. You can't find the enemy, for a start. You get ambushed from time to time in mountains or bogs. Pursuit's a waste of time. All you do is wander around in the rain trying to set fire to things that are too wet to set fire to. (*Silence.*) There's no honour and no satisfaction to be had fighting the Irish.

Silence.

BRITO. I think I could get some satisfaction fighting the Irish. I hear their women are very beautiful.

MORVILLE. The most beautiful I've ever seen.

BRITO. More beautiful than Catherine?

Silence.

More beautiful than Catherine?

MORVILLE. That's a rather stupid question isn't it?

BRITO. Not at all.

MORVILLE. Some are, yes.

BRITO. Some are more beautiful than Catherine?

MORVILLE. Yes. Does that surprise you?

BRITO. Personally, yes. I think there could be no-one more beautiful than Catherine.

Silence.

But I'm asking for your opinion. Do you think –

MORVILLE. Oh for Christ's sake!

BRITO. – I'd have a better time shagging in Ireland than here – shagging Catherine.

MORVILLE *is momentarily shocked but quickly recovers.*

What do you think?

MORVILLE. I think . . . you're trying to provoke me.

BRITO. I try not to waste time on the impossible, Morville!

TRACI. Leave it.

BRITO (*ignoring* TRACI). I'm just wondering whether I'm missing out on a better fuck. What do you think? (*Pause.*) I mean, Catherine's the best I've ever had. Particularly since everybody out there's in awe of her. She's full of herself. Totally uninhibited. A real slut. D'you know what she did to me the other night? I'm lying there with this supernatural hard-on – the kind you get once in a blue moon, the kind you look at and think whose cock is *that?* – and that horny bitch, she got hold of it in both hands, like this –

MORVILLE. Shut up Brito! Shut your nasty, peasant mouth!

BRITO. – and then –

MORVILLE *strikes* BRITO *across the face.* BRITO *stands for a moment with his face to one side, before turning back to* MORVILLE *with a grin.*

Morv' . . . I'm impressed!

MORVILLE *throws his wine into* BRITO*'s face.* BRITO *lunges at* MORVILLE *and they both hit the ground, grappling.* TRACI *starts kicking both of them indiscriminately.*

TRACI. Get up! Get up! Get up!

BRITO. Ow! Ah! Get off! Get off me you old shirt-lifter!

TRACI *stops kicking and stands there looking down at* BRITO. BRITO *stops struggling with the realisation of what's happened.* MORVILLE *quickly gets astride him but* BRITO *has stopped struggling, his head on one side watching* TRACI *as he turns away.*

Traci.

MORVILLE. You little shit! Don't ever talk about her like that again!

BRITO. Yes, yes, sorry Morville. I won't do it again. I promise.

BRITO *disengages himself from* MORVILLE, *rolls to one side and stands. He looks at* TRACI. MORVILLE *is still on his knees.*

Traci. Traci, what's the matter?

TRACI *pours some wine.* MORVILLE *gets to his feet.*

Traci. What's the matter?

TRACI. Nothing.

BRITO. I'm sorry. I shouldn't have . . . In such a trivial way . . .

TRACI. It doesn't matter.

BRITO. It does. I can see it does. But . . . I've always known. And never cared.

MORVILLE. About what?

BRITO (*without looking at him*). Shut up, Morville! I worship the ground you walk on, Traci. You know that. It makes no difference.

There's a desperate note in MORVILLE's *questioning.*

MORVILLE. What doesn't? What are you two talking about?

TRACI. How long have you known?

MORVILLE. Known *what*?

BRITO. Shut up Morville! This is important!

BRITO *steps up to* MORVILLE *and gives him a sharp punch in the solar plexus. He immediately turns back to* TRACI *while* MORVILLE *slowly doubles up.*

I don't know how long. I've just known, but not really known – and not really cared. (*Pause.*) Traci. Come on. How can someone as intelligent as you think I wouldn't know? Of course I've known.

TRACI. Of course. You've known all along that I'm just an old shirt-lifter.

The intensity of TRACI*'s angry stare quickly drives* BRITO *towards panic.*

BRITO. It doesn't matter! It's not important!

TRACI. What's *important* is that I've allowed myself to be pathetically deluded about someone who can think and talk about me in terms of utter contempt.

BRITO *is shattered by the power of* TRACI*'s hostility.*

BRITO. No! . . . No! . . . Forgive me! Traci! Please! I beg you! . . . I'm your friend. There's nothing in my life that gives me more pride than that! . . . Christ it's the *only* thing in my life that gives me pride!

Silence.

Please. Please, Traci. Don't take that away from me. Otherwise . . . there's nothing left for me. Nothing!

TRACI. The fact remains that there's some part of you that sees me as despicable.

BRITO. No! No! Never! Traci . . . Traci . . .

BRITO *throws his arms open in a gesture of desperation. He lowers his head in despair. Then* BRITO *and* TRACI *realise that* MORVILLE *is no longer gasping but sobbing. They watch him for some moments, unsure.*

Morv'. In the name of Christ. What's the matter with you?

MORVILLE. You've hurt me! You've hurt me!

BRITO. It was only a little . . . punch.

MORVILLE. I don't deserve it. I don't deserve it.

MORVILLE *sobs bitterly and abandonedly, on his knees, bent double.*

BRITO. I'm sorry . . . I didn't mean . . .

MORVILLE. It's so awful.

BRITO. Oh no. What? What's so awful Morv'?

MORVILLE. Being here on my own. On my own all the time.

BRITO. But . . . Morv' . . . You're not on your own, Morv', you're –

MORVILLE. Yes I am! It's you two! All the time. You and him. And now you tell me you and her! And there's just *me!* Always just me. And you know that and you enjoy that and . . . it hurts. Sometimes it really hurts . . .

BRITO *is shocked, moved, helpless.*

Traci. Help us.

TRACI (*quietly*). Comfort him.

BRITO *looks at* TRACI *– still cold with humiliation – then turns to the pathetically sobbing* MORVILLE.

BRITO. Morv', look, I . . . Oh Christ! . . . I'm so sorry Morv'. Honestly, I'm really sorry. I'm such a complete and utter cretin sometimes. I've just been too self-centred, too arrogant, to notice, to think . . .

BRITO *is suddenly overwhelmed with pity and remorse.*

Oh Christ I'm so miserable! What a mess. What an almighty fuck-up it all is . . .

BRITO *drops to his knees and embraces* MORVILLE.

Come on Morv', it's alright. I do like you. Of course I like you. So does Traci. And . . . it's a lie. Listen to me. About Catherine. It's a lie. It's all a lie. I've never slept with her. I said it because I'm jealous. I love her. I'm off my head about her. And I'm just jealous. I wanted to hurt you, because . . . she doesn't love me, she loves . . . she loves you, Morville.

A long pause. MORVILLE *looks up at* BRITO, *fearful of being duped.*

It's true. She told me herself.

MORVILLE. Why are you telling me?

BRITO. Because you're a friend and you're upset.

MORVILLE *puts an arm on* BRITO's *shoulder.*

MORVILLE. Thank you. Whether it's true or not. Thank you.

BRITO *turns to look at* TRACI.

BRITO. Look at us. The men who butchered Becket before the altar. In the very gaze of God!

BRITO *holds out a hand.*

Traci. Come on. Please. Please. Come here. Forgive me. Please, Traci.

TRACI *walks over to them, kneels and puts a hand on their shoulders. They stay like this for a few moments before* TRACI *stands up.*

TRACI. Come on, boys. I think it's our bedtime.

BRITO *gets up.*

BRITO. Come on, Morv'.

MORVILLE. No. You go on. I'll stay here for a while.

BRITO *hesitates.*

Don't worry, Brito. I'll be alright. Go on.

BRITO. Goodnight then, Morville.

MORVILLE. Goodnight. Goodnight, Traci.

TRACI. Goodnight.

BRITO *and* TRACI *exit. After a moment or two,* MORVILLE *gets to his feet and goes to the table. He fills a cup with wine, picks up some bread and breaks it into large pieces. He gives the wine and the bread the sign of the cross then goes round to the other side of the table and kneels in prayer for a moment. He stops praying and, staying on his knees, picks up the cup of wine, drinks then picks up a piece of bread and starts to eat. He nearly chokes. He forces it down, then takes a large mouthful of the wine. He picks up another piece of bread and starts to eat and drink – desperately and voraciously.*

Scene Four

December.

Morning. BRITO *enters through the arch followed by* TRACI, *who is carrying* FITZ *on his back.* TRACI *lowers* FITZ *into a chair and turns away to face the fire.*

BRITO (*to* TRACI). Can I get you some breakfast?

TRACI. No thanks, Brito.

FITZ. I'll have some of everything.

BRITO. No, you won't. You're getting too bloody heavy. Nurse and I are putting you on a strict diet. (*Pause.*) Traci. You can't lug him around all day on an empty stomach.

TRACI. I'm fine, Brito. If I'm hungry I'll eat later.

FITZ. I'll have some of everything. Now.

BRITO. I wasn't asking you.

FITZ *grabs* BRITO, *pulling him down face to face.*

FITZ. Then do so!

BRITO *looks into* FITZ's *eyes, shocked by his strength and the intensity of his aggression. The moment is broken by the sound of a hand-bell. They all look at each other in alarm.*

BRITO. Visitors! Fuck – it's Wednesday! Look at the state of the place!

There's a moment of paralysed indecision before they spring into action. BRITO *helps* TRACI *haul* FITZ *onto his back.* TRACI *carries* FITZ *out through the arch. The door opens.* CATHERINE *peers round it, sees the panic and quickly shuts the door.* BRITO *runs over to the fireplace, picks up a bucket and throws water onto the fire, nearly extinguishing it.* TRACI *rushes back on through the arch and tidies the table before they both rush downstage and kneel together at prayer, facing the audience. There's a knock at the door and it opens slowly to reveal* CATHERINE, *carrying a basket.* CATHERINE *enters, followed by a middle-aged man (called* JOHN, *known as the* VISITOR). TRACI *and* BRITO *start quietly mouthing any old nonsense to give*

the impression of praying. CATHERINE *motions the*
VISITOR *to stay by the door then takes a chair and places
it next to him. She gestures 'Sit down. No talking.'*

The VISITOR *sits.* CATHERINE *takes Christmas
decorations from the basket and starts putting them up. She
seems weary in her movements. She has a persistent cough.*

CATHERINE. The knights spend their day in prayer and
fasting, eating once after sunset.

TRACI. Bibbly bobbly, bibbly bobbly, bibbly bobbly . . .

BRITO. Becket was a wanker he deserved all he got, Becket was
a wanker he deserved all he got. Becket was a wanker . . .
Amen.

Silence.

Only one! We've never had just one before.

TRACI. We made history. Now we are history.

BRITO. One! Not worth spoiling your breakfast for.

Silence.

That was scary just now.

TRACI. What?

BRITO. Fitz! If he gets on his feet he'll be dangerous. I know it.

TRACI. Why should he be dangerous?

BRITO. Because we crippled him. And because he's Fitz. We
should chain him to the wall.

CATHERINE. There are always two knights at prayer day and
night. They allow themselves only four hours sleep at a
time.

TRACI. Bibbly bobbly, bibbly bobbly, bibbly bobbly . . .

BRITO. Becket was a wanker he deserved all he got, Becket
was a wanker he deserved all he got . . .

TRACI. I think he's changed.

BRITO. He'll never change.

TRACI. He is doing. Morally as well as physically.

BRITO. Fitz!?

TRACI. Why not? <u>Why shouldn't Knaresborough be Fitz's</u> <u>road to Damascus?</u>

BRITO. Oh yes. Why not? Anything's possible round here!

TRACI. <u>He will walk again. But not until his suffering has</u> <u>become equal to the weight of his sins. That's when he'll be</u> <u>able to forgive himself. And that's when he'll walk.</u>

BRITO *stares at* TRACI *with deep concern.*

BRITO. Physician, heal thyself! I'm on my own here. Fitz thinks he's Lazarus. You think he's St Paul. Morville thinks Becket is alive and well – and living in Knaresborough! He sleeps most nights under that table – pissed as a rat and covered in breadcrumbs!

Silence.

TRACI. Morville is unstable.

BRITO. Unstable? He's completely fucking mad!

VISITOR (*to* CATHERINE, *shocked*). What did he say?

CATHERINE *ignores him.*

(*Insistent.*) Did you hear what he said?

CATHERINE: Yes. (*Struggling.*) He said 'Forgive me . . . '

VISITOR. No he didn't.

CATHERINE. 'Forgive me for being so . . .'

VISITOR. Yes? For being so what?

CATHERINE (*losing patience*). ' . . . fucking bad!'

VISITOR. What!

CATHERINE. <u>These men are soldiers! In their fight for</u> <u>salvation they sometimes use the language of the battlefield.</u>

Pause.

VISITOR. Are you trying to be funny?

TRACI. Oh for God's sake!

TRACI *gets to his feet.*

I'm sorry, Catherine. (*Pause. To* VISITOR.) I'm William de Traci. This is Richard le Bret. What's your name?

VISITOR. John.

TRACI. Catherine, would you pour our guest a drink?

CATHERINE *pours some wine and gives it to the* VISITOR.

VISITOR. Thank you.

She resumes decorating.

TRACI. Curious about us were you, John?

VISITOR *hesitates.*

VISITOR. Well –

BRITO. So what do you think? First impressions and all that. I'm quite good-looking, don't you think?

VISITOR. Well –

BRITO. Now Traci, he looks intelligent doesn't he?

VISITOR. Well –

BRITO. This man is one of the best brains in Europe. And one of the best fighters. You're in the presence of greatness, John! Tell him about yourself, Traci. Give him his money's worth. Would you like Traci to tell you about himself, John?

VISITOR. Well –

BRITO. Of course you would. Go on Traci, give him your CV.

TRACI. Well, John. I was born into middle-ranking aristocracy, trained as a soldier, then got religion – well not religion so much as curiosity, a need to learn and to think about things on a daily basis. I studied theology in Paris then spent four years in a monastery. It was a worthwhile, well-run organisation doing useful work. I enjoyed it. I left for one reason. I didn't fancy spending my middle years in love with one pretty little novice after another. I'd remained celibate but I knew it was only a matter of time before I lost my heart and my head to some golden haired beauty with dark blue eyes. And then, probably, sooner or later, the decline into sex. A life revolving around brief bouts of buggery. Orgasm followed by guilt and emptiness. Over and over again. The most repetitive, pointless life imaginable as I've no doubt you'd agree, John. So I joined the crusaders for a change of scene. When I became tired of sporadic slaughter and a war that was unwinnable, I got involved in

negotiations with the Islamics, earned a reputation as a
bruiser with a brain and was eventually appointed to the
royal household. (*Pause.*) Clear so far?

VISITOR. Well, yes . . .

BRITO. What else do you want to know?

Silence.

TRACI. Come on, John. You must want to know something.

VISITOR. Well . . . yes. (*Pause.*) *Why?* Why did you do it?

CATHERINE *stops decorating.*

TRACI. Good question, John. Good question. I'm not really
sure any more. Brito might know. Brito? Can you tell John
why we did it?

BRITO. Yes. It's very simple, John. But first you need the
background. Last year Henry decided to have his eldest son
crowned king of England. His reasons: one, to ensure
succession for his son; two, to establish continuity and
stability; and three, to allow Henry to concentrate on
Europe while his son practises kingship on England – a
damp, dark, poxy little country that Henry has never liked
anyway. But your traditional English coronation requires
the Archbishop of Canterbury. And there isn't one. Becket's
gone AWOL. He's been sulking on the continent for years
and refusing to come into work. But the boy's coronation
is very important to Henry. He asks Becket 'Come back,
officiate at the coronation and let's be friends again.'
Becket, being Becket, refused. Henry, being Henry, made
do with some other Bishops. All the top men. York, London,
Salisbury, Chester, Durham – they were all there to give the
boy their blessing. So now his son's in place to take over
and Henry is feeling mellow and just tired – tired of all this
Becket bullshit. He decides to give in! He tells Becket
'Okay, you can have virtually everything you demand and
the rest we can sort out between us in a spirit of
reconciliation. Let's start again. Return to Canterbury, and
let's just start again'. What does Becket do? In the hour of
his victory? Returns to England, yes – but his first official
act on English soil? He excommunicates the Bishops of
York, London, Salisbury, Chester and Durham! Thereby

invalidating the coronation. Now *that* was cheeky. Henry has just placed the crown on his son's head and Becket snatches it off. *That* is treason. Treason pure and simple. But what's more, John, *it's taking the piss*. To an awesome degree. We're with Henry in Normandy, Christmas Day. Everybody's enjoying themselves when Henry suddenly goes ballistic. We're standing around dumbstruck thinking 'What the fuck's the matter with him all of a sudden?' Some twat of a messenger's arrived, told him Becket's confirmed the excommunications and he's been roaming southern England at the head of a small army. Henry says get over to Canterbury, tell that lunatic to reinstate the coronation bishops and if he refuses, arrest him. We get to Canterbury, we go and see Becket. We go to the bishops palace, unarmed, and ask for a few minutes of his valuable time. No problem. He says 'Join me for lunch, lads.' We said 'Well that would be very pleasant, your grace, but the occasion would be more pleasant if we cleared up a couple of points beforehand.' 'And what may they be?' 'Will you reinstate the coronation bishops?' 'Fuck off,' says his grace. We told him we had a warrant for his arrest. 'Fuck off.' And we did: we were unarmed and outnumbered. We went away, tooled up, came back. He'd gone to the cathedral. We found him, tried to arrest him, he resisted, things got badly out of hand, and he died. And that's it, John.

Silence.

VISITOR. Just like that.

BRITO. Exactly like that.

TRACI. He's telling you the truth as he knows it, John. What *happened*. But you asked *why*. Much more interesting, *much* more difficult. *Why*, for instance, did Becket go to the cathedral, virtually alone, totally unprotected, when he knew we would do our best to arrest him. (*Pause.*) One answer, John: he went there because it was the perfect stage for his own martyrdom. That's what he wanted. Martyrdom. And we . . . were stupid enough to oblige.

VISITOR. Oh I see. *You're* the victims.

BRITO. Don't push it, John.

TRACI. We were Becket's victims in the degree to which you accept he made us his accomplices rather than his assassins.

BRITO *and* VISITOR, *both baffled, stare at* TRACI.
BRITO *suddenly turns to* VISITOR.

BRITO. See? Listen and learn, John. *Don't* take the piss.

TRACI. Even more interesting to me now is why it all seemed
  so inevitable. I knew what was going to happen. And I knew
  it was madness. But I was powerless. Caught in a current.
  And of course you only notice it when it's too late. You
  think you're swimming, striking out this way or that, in a
  huge lake. But suddenly you realise you're not. You're in a
  powerful, fast-flowing river – it's just that you can't see the
  banks. Do you see, John? History had made up its mind.
  Not us. Not Becket. Not Henry, even. He knew that. That's
  why he was so angry when he sent us over. He was
  surrendering to the tyranny of history.

TRACI *sighs and smiles.*

The fact is no-one will ever know why we did it.

MORVILLE *appears in the archway, holding a drink in his
hand. The others watch him in silence as he walks
unsteadily towards the table.*

This is our host, John. Hugh de Morville.

MORVILLE *stops and stares at* VISITOR.

MORVILLE: Christ! Is it Wednesday?

MORVILLE *staggers.* TRACI *attempts to hold him up, but*
MORVILLE *slides to the ground.*

CATHERINE. That's all the time the knights will allow, I'm
  afraid. They don't wish to be distracted further from their
  devotions.

VISITOR. Devotions my arse! (*Pause.*) Look, I came here to
  tell you something . . .

He pauses, scared by BRITO*'s look of aggression.*

TRACI. You're in no danger from us, John. Say what you want
  to say.

VISITOR. Right. Okay. Right . . . Right . . . Ever since you
  arrived this town's seen nothing but trouble. We've had the
  coldest winters and the worst harvest in living memory.
  Now there's sickness in the town. People are dying. My
  sister-in-law died three nights ago.

BRITO. You can't blame us for that!

VISITOR. I don't! I'm not bloody stupid. I don't blame you for any of that. (*Pause.*) Even the massacre. Anybody with any sense knows it must've been you who slaughtered Wigmore and his crew. I lost two cousins that night. Hotheads and trouble-makers the pair of them. I don't give a toss. Good riddance. Even my sister-in-law – Margaret – woman of your close acqaintance I believe – poor brainless bitch was just a bloody embarrassment! None of that gives me a problem. What matters to me is . . . *wool!*

Silence.

TRACI. Wool . . .

VISITOR. Trade! Business! Wool's my living and the wool trade's going to ratshit – like every other business round here. (*To* BRITO.) Look! Whether he's a great man or just a queer up shit creek doesn't matter. (*To* TRACI.) It doesn't matter whether history's a lake, a river or a bloody duck-pond! You lot. The king. Becket. It doesn't matter. What matters is that people *do business!*

Silence.

Your presence fills this town with the stench of . . . failure!

A groan from MORVILLE.

MORVILLE. We're sorry. We're so sorry.

VISITOR *looks down at* MORVILLE, *exasperated.*

VISITOR. It's bloody pathetic is this! (*To* TRACI.) Go! No-one cares any more. Just go! (*To* CATHERINE.) And you should go with them. You may be blessed. You may be a healer. But you're part of this pantomime, aren't you!

BRITO *grabs* VISITOR *by the throat.*

BRITO. If you speak to her or to my friend in that tone of voice again I will throw you out the window.

VISITOR (*gasps*). You bloody won't!

BRITO. John, I bloody will.

BRITO *very slowly forces* VISITOR *onto his knees, throttling him.*

TRACI. Leave him.

BRITO *thrusts* VISITOR *aside in disgust.* VISITOR *stays on his knees fighting for breath.*

CATHERINE. Come on.

VISITOR *gets up, staggering, and* CATHERINE *leads him to the door.* CATHERINE *and* VISITOR *exit. There's a long, depressed silence.* TRACI *is deep in thought.* BRITO *watches him.*

MORVILLE. We're sorry. We really are.

BRITO. No we are not! You stupid piss-head!

TRACI *groans, gets* MORVILLE *to his feet and takes him out through the archway.* BRITO *pours some wine and puts the cup on the table without drinking from it. He picks up a big log and throws it onto the fire.* CATHERINE *re-enters. She begins decorating where she left off.* BRITO *watches her for a while.*

Don't you ever stop working?

He watches her.

You look beautiful today.

CATHERINE. Thank you.

BRITO. Are you going to give me a Christmas present?

CATHERINE. What would you like?

BRITO. A fuck.

Silence.

I want to hold your face in my hands and kiss you as you come. (*Pause.*) Can I have that? Just once before I leave?

CATHERINE. No.

Silence.

CATHERINE. When are you going?

BRITO. In a couple of weeks. Maybe. Maybe not 'til the Spring. God knows.

Silence.

Has he done it yet?

CATHERINE. Done what?

BRITO. Asked you to marry him.

CATHERINE. No.

BRITO. Git. (*Pause.*) Never mind, Catherine. He will. He does love you. Pity he's turned into an alcoholic madman, though, isn't it?

CATHERINE. He'll get better.

BRITO. You're as bad as Traci. People don't get better, they get worse! They don't get stronger, they get weaker! They don't get younger, they get older!

Silence.

My god what an education this place has been. (*Pause.*) Fitz loves Traci. Traci loves me. Morville and I love you. (*Pause.*) And you? Who knows?

Silence. CATHERINE *stops working and drops her head, gasping.*

What's the matter?

She becomes momentarily unsteady. He moves close to her but doesn't touch her.

What's the matter?

CATHERINE. I don't know.

BRITO *puts a hand to her forehead.*

BRITO. Christ! You're burning. (*Pause.*) You've got a fever.

CATHERINE. Yes.

BRITO. How long?

CATHERINE. I'm not sure.

BRITO. Hours? Days?

CATHERINE. Days.

BRITO. Days!

He stares into her face with a terrible realisation.

You've been going in there, haven't you? Amongst the sick.

CATHERINE *nods.*

(*Angry.*) Why? You haven't got over the last time they tried kill you!

CATHERINE. They begged me. <u>Because I'm blessed. I had no choice!</u>

BRITO *is hit by a wave of love and fear.*

BRITO. Oh no. No.

BRITO *puts his arms around her. She remains impassive. He tries to kiss her.*

CATHERINE. No!

She pulls away. BRITO *looks at her, hopeless and immensely sad. She half reaches out to touch him.*

I don't want to kill you.

BRITO. Then just tell me you love me.

CATHERINE. No.

He bows his head, crushed with misery. He looks up. He suddenly takes hold of her shoulders.

BRITO. Then kill me.

They're still for a moment. Then BRITO *slowly moves forward and kisses her with exquisite tenderness. They fall to their knees as she fades into semi-consciousness. He goes on kissing her with the same tenderness. He stops and looks at her, limp in his arms.* TRACI *enters by the arch. He stops when he sees* BRITO *and* CATHERINE.

TRACI. Excuse me.

TRACI *turns to go.*

BRITO. Traci. (*Pause.*) We need a priest.

TRACI. What for?

BRITO *picks up* CATHERINE *and stands.*

BRITO. Morville's getting married.

BRITO *carries her out through the arch.*

Scene Five

Several hours later. It's night. TRACI *is alone in the room. From off there's a loud scream of terror fading quickly to silence. A few seconds later* BRITO *enters through the arch.*

TRACI. Who was that?

BRITO. The priest. Morville and I just threw him off the top.

BRITO *sits down by the table.* TRACI *looks disapproving but says nothing.*

We've done an archbishop, Traci, so what's a parish priest between friends?

Pause.

TRACI. Did she go easily?

BRITO. When Morville told her he was adopting her son she was radiant. Right to the end.

TRACI. Where's Morville?

BRITO. He's with the boy. Waiting for him to go to sleep.

TRACI. Does the boy know?

BRITO. No.

BRITO *gives a sudden, stifled sob.*

Oh . . . Traci. Traci. Go down there and see her. See how beautiful she looks.

Silence.

I'll be alright. (*Pause.*) Part of me feels relieved. (*Long pause.*) I'm leaving. Come with me. Please.

TRACI. We must all leave together. When Fitz can walk.

BRITO. No. I don't need Fitz.

TRACI. Yes! You do. We all have to face the Pope. When that moment comes the only thing that will give us strength and even a shred of credibilty is loyalty. To Henry. And to *each other.* We must go to Rome *together.* We must face the Pope *together*.

Silence.

We're soldiers, Brito. We must *hold!* At the centre.

BRITO. But I'm so sick of the waiting! And these nights. These terrible, endless nights.

FITZ *appears in the arch. He stands there, confident, leaner yet somehow enlarged and more powerful.*

TRACI. It's complete. You're healed!

FITZ. Yes. Impressive, isn't it? I was in there just now and there was this blinding light and a voice said 'On your feet, Fitz! Walk!' And I did.

TRACI. You're not serious?

FITZ. No.

FITZ *approaches* BRITO.

Is she dead?

BRITO *just returns the stare.*

TRACI. Yes.

FITZ *nods, turns away from* BRITO *and walks up to* TRACI, *smiling.* FITZ *knees* TRACI *in the balls. As* TRACI *drops,* BRITO *moves towards* FITZ.

FITZ. Wait!

BRITO *checks, momentarily, and* FITZ *punches* BRITO, *winding him, and then smashes his head into the table.* FITZ *takes out a cord and ties* BRITO*'s hands behind his back.* MORVILLE *appears in the arch.*

MORVILLE. Oh Christ. You're back.

FITZ. Morville. Come in. Join us.

FITZ *takes out a garotte and puts it over* BRITO*'s head.*

Oh and congratulations! Husband, father and widower in one day. Good going, Morville.

MORVILLE *approaches* FITZ, *picking up a sword.*

MORVILLE. Let go of him.

FITZ. Not a chance.

TRACI. Back off for now Morville. I think he's got something he needs to say.

MORVILLE *hesitates then nods.*

MORVILLE. But another crack like that – even mention her name – and I swear to god I'll cut your throat as you sleep.

MORVILLE *turns away and heads for the chair by the fire.*

FITZ (*impressed*). Well! What a day for surprises!

BRITO *groans, recovering consciousness.*

Now. Where was I? Oh yes!

FITZ *pulls* BRITO *upright onto his knees. He twists* BRITO*'s head back and looks down into his eyes.*

I've been exercising for weeks in there! Weeks! Ask me if I've loved every minute of it.

FITZ *kicks* BRITO.

BRITO. Fuck yourself, Fitz!

FITZ *kicks him again.*

FITZ. Ask me!

A brief pause. BRITO *turns angrily to* TRACI.

BRITO. I told you!

FITZ *hits him.*

FITZ. Ask me!

TRACI. Do it!

BRITO *smiles contemptuously.*

BRITO. Did you love every *minute* of it, shithead?

FITZ. Well, since you ask . . .

FITZ *grips* BRITO *by the hair and stares into his eyes.*

Yes I fucking did!! (*Pause.*) Now. I'm not doing this just to teach a *boy* not to get into a pissing contest with *men!* (*Pause.*) Truth is . . . I'm in a deeply confused state. And I want help. And I want to be taken seriously. If not I'll get upset. And as we all know, when I get upset usually someone dies. In this case *him!* (*Pause.*) At the heart of my confusion is one simple question. (*Pause.*) Does God exist?

FITZ *stares at* TRACI, *waiting. Silence.*

I'm serious, Traci. Does God exist?

TRACI. No.

FITZ. What do you mean 'no'?

TRACI. First . . . I ask *you* a question.

FITZ. You're in no position to make demands.

TRACI. Yes I am. Whatever you want it's not to kill Brito or you would've done it.

FITZ. One question.

TRACI. Why did you kill Becket?

FITZ. We'll come to that. I promise you. But *first* . . .

    FITZ *tightens the garotte.*

    Does God exist?

TRACI. I believe so.

FITZ. Why do you believe so? And if I even hear the word 'faith' . . .

TRACI. Apart from the word you've just mentioned –

    FITZ *pulls on the garotte.* BRITO *chokes.*

FITZ. I'm in charge of smartarse, superior humour tonight! – and I've decided there won't be any.

    BRITO *cracks. He slumps forward, sobbing.*

    Well, well –

TRACI. Fitz! You can only take this so far –

FITZ. I'll take it as far as I like! Until I get what I want.

TRACI. What do you want?

FITZ. Some truth and some *peace!*

TRACI. There's no peace in truth. And no truth in peace.

FITZ. Ohh . . . ! So where does that leave us? (*To* BRITO.) See what we're up against? A knife at your throat and that's the best our theologian can do. Another empty paradox – meaning *nothing!*

TRACI. Finally there *is* no meaning. Only belief. And there's no belief without courage.

FITZ. Oh he just can't help himself, can he? Reasons! I want reasons! Tell me *why* you believe!

TRACI. Because I *look* at the world around me.

FITZ. And see what?

TRACI. That the world is *saturated* with God!

FITZ. Too thin, Traci. Too *thin!*

TRACI. That's all I can give you.

FITZ. *Try . . . harder.*

> FITZ *tightens the garotte.*

TRACI (*wearily*). Everything has a cause. Everything changes. There has to be something which began it all. A first cause. And something which doesn't change. Some constant against chaos. The heart of things. That is God.

FITZ. Why does there have to be a first cause?

TRACI. If there's no first cause there must be infinite regress. Infinite regress is an absurdity. (*Pause.*) Think about . . . an inverted pyramid. It can have any number of stones, be any size, is capable of infinite growth, but at the bottom, at the start, there must be that single stone. That first stone was put there by God. And is *held there* by God. He's there. At the bottom of everything. Permanent and unchanging.

FITZ. Why unchanging?

TRACI. Because God is perfect. He cannot change.

FITZ. But we can?

TRACI. Yes.

FITZ. You're telling me I have greater freedom than God.

TRACI. Yes.

FITZ. But it isn't freedom that I want!

TRACI. What do you want?

FITZ. I want . . . to stop looking at the world and feeling as if I'm standing in front of . . . a beautiful door, but that on the other side of that door is a cold, dark, empty room.

TRACI. We're all afraid of death, Fitz. Faith or no faith.

FITZ. No! That's not it. It's . . . the injustice. At the back of everything. The senselessness. (*Pause, to* BRITO.) You think you're suffering. Because a woman you're infatuated with has died. Watch a *child* die! *Your* child! Your heart! Ripped out of you!

FITZ *stares hard at* TRACI.

When my son was dying . . . I knew there'd be pain . . . not *such* pain, not for so long, but I knew there'd be pain . . . but . . . but not the rage. The *rage!*

TRACI. Fitz –

FITZ. No! Don't say anything! Listen!

Silence. FITZ *can hardly speak through his rage.*

I loathed Becket. Long before he betrayed Henry. Detested him. And that's always been reason enough for me to kill someone. But *not* the Archbishop of Canterbury, in public, in his cathedral. Even I know you can't get away with something that crazy. But . . . I killed him. And I felt so good. So fulfilled. Deep inside so . . . *just!* (*Pause.*) I'd gone to that cathedral, like you, all of us, to arrest an archbishop. But once inside the place I was doing something else. I wasn't looking for Becket – I was looking for God. I wanted to find him . . . and hurt him. (*Pause.*) Killing Becket was as near as I could get . . . to killing God.

Silence.

MORVILLE. Christ. You really are insane.

FITZ *jabs his knife at the ceiling.*

FITZ. I don't care *who* He is, Morville! Letting children die in pain *isn't fucking good enough!* Letting *my* child die in pain is *un-for-givable!!*

Silence.

(*To* TRACI.) So tell me. *Am* I insane?

TRACI *doesn't reply.*

I must be. Because I still want to believe that God exists. That he's taking care of my son. And that when I die God can forgive me for just one moment – just one moment when I can pick up that beautiful, beautiful child and hold

him . . . hold him . . . his arms around my neck, his eyes
smiling into mine . . .

*FITZ is still and silent for a while. Then he begins to weep.
After a few moments he stops and gives a cry of enormous
pain. He pulls back* BRITO*'s head.*

Every day I feel that little boy's pain and despair more
deeply than *you* . . . will ever feel *anything!*

FITZ drops to his knees beside BRITO, *weeping loudly. The
others are silent while* FITZ *slowly regains control of
himself.*

TRACI. And God shall wipe away the tears from his eyes and
there shall be no more death, neither sorrow nor crying,
neither shall there be any more pain. God will make all
things new.

FITZ stares desolately at TRACI.

FITZ. You believe that?

TRACI. Most days.

Pause.

FITZ. *Most* days?

TRACI. Yes.

FITZ. *You* doubt?

TRACI. Of course I doubt! There's doubt in all of us! There
has to be –

FITZ. Why?

TRACI. – or we wouldn't be free. God made us free – and
keeps himself at a distance.

FITZ. But *why?*

TRACI. So we remain free! So we're not overwhelmed by his
presence! If he were there in front of us, even if there were
just some kind of proof, life would be impossible for us.
There would be no choices. Nothing would matter. (*Pause.*)
It's the mystery that gives life meaning.

Silence. No-one moves.

MORVILLE. I'll explain that to the boy. When I tell him his
mother's dead.

Silence. MORVILLE *is suddenly on his feet, the sword in
his hand, poised over* FITZ.

(*To* FITZ.) You mad, sick *fuck!* All this. Because of you.
Everything I ever believed in or ever wanted – in ruins!

FITZ, *still on his knees, looks up at* MORVILLE.

FITZ (*softly, quietly*). Forgive me.

MORVILLE. Not a chance.

MORVILLE *spits in* FITZ'*s face and raises the sword.* FITZ
doesn't move, and fixes MORVILLE *in an unflinching stare.*

A little BOY, *about eight, wearing a nightdress, appears in
the archway. No-one notices him.*

FITZ. Kill me. Or forgive me.

A moment's hesitation then MORVILLE *raises the sword.*

BRITO. Morville! Not in front the boy.

MORVILLE *looks round and sees the* BOY. *He groans,
drops the sword and goes and picks him up. The* BOY *puts
his arms round* MORVILLE'*s neck.* MORVILLE *sits in
front of the fire with the child on his lap.*

The others look at the child in silence. The BOY *looks back
at them, solemn and defiant.*

TRACI *takes the knife from* FITZ'*s hand and cuts* BRITO'*s
bindings.*

TRACI. We'll leave as soon as we find a priest for the burial.
(*Pause.*) Let's go. Let's go and see the Pope.

BRITO *gets to his feet.*

BRITO. Just *one* thing.

BRITO *picks up the sword.*

No-one . . .

BRITO *rams the sword into the floor in front of* FITZ.

. . . kills the old bastard!

A brief silence before a drumbeat emerges. TRACI *kneels alongside* FITZ. *After a few moments,* BRITO *kneels alongside* TRACI. *They wait.* MORVILLE *stands, lowers the* BOY *into the chair, walks across to the group and kneels. They all raise their right hands and clasp the sword beneath the handle so that they appear to be holding aloft a cross, their heads bowed in prayer.*

TRACI. The King!

FITZ. The King!

MORVILLE. The King!

BRITO. The King!

ALL. The King!!

As the stage begins to darken, the BOY *leaves the chair and walks towards the closed circle of knights.* MORVILLE *holds out an arm, opening the circle. The* BOY *stops. Then he walks into the circle and it closes round him, leaving the* BOY's *head and shoulders standing clear in the centre, back to the audience. He puts out a hand on each side as if to embrace the figures kneeling around him. Then he, too, bows his head. The drums climax and cease. Simultaneously, the stained-glass rose-window bursts into light, bathing the* BOY *and the* KNIGHTS *in colour and silence.*